Literary Sources for Roman Britain

Fifth Edition

LACTOR Sourcebooks in Ancient History

For more than half a century, *LACTOR Sourcebooks in Ancient History* have been providing for the needs of students at schools and universities who are studying ancient history in English translation. Each volume focuses on a particular period or topic and offers a generous and judicious selection of primary texts in new translations. The texts selected include not only extracts from important literary sources but also numerous inscriptions, coin legends and extracts from legal and other texts, which are not otherwise easy for students to access. Many volumes include annotation as well as a glossary, maps and other relevant illustrations, and sometimes a short Introduction. The volumes are written and reviewed by experienced teachers of ancient history at both schools and universities. The series is now being published in print and digital form by Cambridge University Press, with plans for both new editions and completely new volumes.

Osborne	*The Athenian Empire*
Osborne	*The Old Oligarch*
Cooley	*Cicero's Consulship Campaign*
Grocock	*Inscriptions of Roman Britain*
Osborne	*Athenian Democracy*
Santangelo	*Late Republican Rome, 88-31 BC*
Warmington/Miller	*Inscriptions of the Roman Empire, AD 14-117*
Treggiari	*Cicero's Cilician Letters*
Rathbone/Rathbone	*Literary Sources for Roman Britain*
Sabben-Clare/Warman	*The Culture of Athens*
Stockton	*From the Gracchi to Sulla*
Edmondson	*Dio: the Julio-Claudians*
Brosius	*The Persian Empire from Cyrus II to Artaxerxes I*
Cooley/Wilson	*The Age of Augustus*
Levick	*The High Tide of Empire*
Cooley	*Tiberius to Nero*
Cooley	*The Flavians*
Cooley	*Sparta*

Literary Sources for Roman Britain

Fifth Edition

Edited by
YVETTE RATHBONE

and

D. W. RATHBONE
King's College London

 CAMBRIDGE
UNIVERSITY PRESS

CAMBRIDGE
UNIVERSITY PRESS

Shaftesbury Road, Cambridge CB2 8EA, United Kingdom

One Liberty Plaza, 20th Floor, New York, NY 10006, USA

477 Williamstown Road, Port Melbourne, VIC 3207, Australia

314–321, 3rd Floor, Plot 3, Splendor Forum, Jasola District Centre, New Delhi – 110025, India

103 Penang Road, #05–06/07, Visioncrest Commercial, Singapore 238467

Cambridge University Press is part of Cambridge University Press & Assessment, a department of the University of Cambridge.

We share the University's mission to contribute to society through the pursuit of education, learning and research at the highest international levels of excellence.

www.cambridge.org
Information on this title: www.cambridge.org/9781009383219
DOI: 10.1017/9781009383240

First published 2023

A catalogue record for this publication is available from the British Library.

A Cataloging-in-Publication data record for this book is available from the Library of Congress.

ISBN 978-1-009-38321-9 Paperback

TABLE OF CONTENTS

PREFACE AND ACKNOWLEDGEMENTS

This fourth edition of *Literary Sources for Roman Britain* has four main purposes: most importantly it keeps in print the version of texts prescribed for A-level Ancient History within the UK. In addition long texts on Caesar's invasions of Britain by Cassius Dio and by Caesar himself have been newly translated, though Tacitus' *Agricola*, easily available in various translations, is not included. Earlier editions arranged the texts by date of composition. This edition returns to the more normal arrangement of grouping texts according to the historical events being written about. Finally it also includes more in the way of historical notes than previous editions.

Yvette Rathbone undertook the large task of re-ordering and re-formatting the material and also translating passages from Caesar's *Gallic Wars*. Dominic Rathbone translated Dio's account of Caesar's invasions and has been responsible for the bulk of the historical notes. I am very grateful to them for all their efforts and expertise, and to Andrew Harvey for his efficiency in printing the book. We hope the material will be clear and useful but shall be grateful to hear of mistakes or suggestions for improvements.

M.G.L. Cooley
LACTOR General Editor,
Head of Scholars, Warwick School
June 2012

SOURCES AND PASSAGES

Brief details are given here for sources quoted in more than one section; for the other sources, the relevant information is given with the passage cited **in bold**.

Ammianus Marcellinus, *History* 14.5.6–9 (V1); 18.2.3 (V2.3); 20.1.1–3 (V4); 26.4.5 (W1); 27.8.1–10 (W2.1); 28.3.1–9 (W2.2); 29.4.7 (W2.5); 30.7.3 (U2).

> A 4th-century officer who wrote (in Latin) a mainly military history of the Empire in his own day, but starting in AD 96. Books 13–31 survive, which cover AD 353–378.

Anonymus Valesianus 2.4 (S2.2).

Appian, *Roman History* preface.5 (J3).

Augustus, *Res Gestae* 32.1 (**B4.1**).

Aurelius Victor, *Caesars* 20.18 (N3.7), 20.27 (N4.2); 39.40–41 (R1.2).

> A senator of the mid-4th century who wrote brief biographies of the emperors from Augustus to Constantius II.

Caesar, *Gallic Wars* 4.20–22 (A1), 4.23–27 (A2), 4.28–32 (A3), 4.33–38 (A4); 5.1–7 (A5), 5.8–9 (A6), 5.10–11 (A7), 5.12–14 (A16), 5.15–19 (A8), 5.20–21 (A9), 5.22–23 (A10); 6.11, 13–16 (A17).

> Gaius Julius Caesar, consul in 59 BC, campaigned in Gaul from 58 to 49 BC, when he used his army and wealth from booty to launch a civil war. His account of his campaigns is a much expanded version of the reports Roman generals were meant to send to the Senate, which he seems to have published in annual instalments to advertise his successes and justify his unauthorised actions, such as invading Britain. His account is written in a deceptively plain and lucid style, including the use of the third person to make it seem more objective.

Cassius Dio, *Roman History* 39.50–53 (A12.1); 40.1–4 (A12.2); 49.38.2 (B2.1); 53.22.5 (B2.2), 53.25.2 (B2.3); 55.23.2–5 (O1.1); 59.25.1–3 (D2.2); 60.19.1–3 (E3.1), 60.19.4–5 (E3.2), 60.20.1–4 (E4), 60.20.5–6 (E5.1), 60.21.1–5 (E5.2), 60.22.1–2 (E7.2);
(Dio-Xiphilinus) 60.23.1–6 (E7.3), 60.30.2 (E7.6); 62.1.1.–3.4 (F3.5), 62.7.1.–9.2 (F3.6), 62.12.1–6 (F3.7); 66.20.1–3 (H1.1); 69.13.2 (J4); 71.16.2 (L1.3); 72.8.1 (M1), 72.9.2ᵃ (M2.3), 72.9.2² (M2.4); 73.14.3 (N1.1), 73.15.1 (N1.2); 75.4.1 (N1.3), 75.5.4 (N3.1); 76.10.6 (N3.2), 76.11.1 (N3.3), 76.12.1–5 (N2.2), 76.13.1–4 (N3.6), 76.15.1 (N3.9), 76.15.2–3 (N4.5); 77.1.1 (O1.2).

> Cassius Dio Cocceianus, a Greek aristocrat who became a senator in the reign of Commodus and was twice consul under the Severan dynasty, wrote a history

(in Greek) of Rome from its foundation to his own day. Only the books covering 69 BC to AD 46 are extant in full. The rest survive only in citations by Byzantine authors, especially the Epitome (summary) of books 36–80 made by the 11th-century monk Joannes Xiphilinus, who sometimes garbled Dio's text.

Chronicler of 452 under 382 (**X1**).

Cicero, *Letters to Atticus* 4.15.10 (**A11.1**), 4.16.7 (**A11.2**), 4.18.5 (**A11.3**).

Claudian, *On the Fourth Consulship of Honorius* 23–24 (**W2.4**); *On the Consulship of Stilicho* 2.247–255 (**Y1.1**); *On the Gothic War* 404–18 (**Y1.2**).

Claudian, from Alexandria, lived in Italy in the early 5th century and wrote poems in Latin, including praises of Honorius and his court.

Council of Arles Mansi II 476 (**T1**).

Digest 1.19.2 (F3.3); 36.1.48 (H3).

The Digest is a massive compilation of Roman legal principles and rulings collated by the order of the emperor Justinian and published in AD 533.

Diodorus Siculus, *Library* 5.21.1–22.1 (**A15**).

Epitome of the Caesars 41.3 (**S2.1**).

Eunapius fragment 12 (**V2.2**).

Eutropius, *Brief History* 7.13.2–3 (E2.2); 8.19.1 (N3.8); 9.21–22 (R1.1).

A court official of the later 4th century AD who wrote an outline history (in Latin) of Rome from its foundation to AD 364.

Firmicius Maternus, *On the Errors of Profane Religions* 28.6 (**U1**).

Frontinus, *Stratagems* 2.13.11 (**A14**).

Fronto, *Letter to Marcus on the Parthian War (Loeb II p.20)* 2 (**J1.2**).

Herodian, *History* 3.7.1 (N1.4), 3.8.2 (N1.5); 3.14.1–5 (N3.4), 3.14.6–8 (N2.1), 3.14.9–10 (N3.5); 3.15.1–8 (N4.6).

Herodian, probably an imperial freedman of the earlier 3rd century, wrote (in Greek) a history of the period AD 180–238, which is of variable quality.

Historia Augusta (HA), *Hadrian* 5.1–2 (J1.1), 11.2 (J2); *Antoninus Pius* 5.4 (K1.1); *Marcus* 8.7 (L1.1), 22.1 (L1.2); *Commodus* 6.1–2 (M2.1), 8.4 (M2.2);

Pertinax 2.1 (M3.1), 3.5–10 (M3.2); *Severus* 19.1 (N4.3), 22.4 (N4.1), 23.3 (N4.4).

The 'Augustan History' is a collection of biographies of all the Emperors and Caesars, including failed usurpers, from Hadrian to Carinus (AD 117–284) by an unknown author of the late 4th century who uses six pseudonyms. Although the later and minor biographies are almost fiction, the earlier ones (including those used here) seem more reliable, and probably drew heavily on the imperial biographies of Marius Maximus, a senator of the Severan period.

Horace, *Odes* 1.35.29–30 (B2.4); 3.5.1–4 (**B2.5**).

Josephus, *Jewish War* 3.4–5 (**E6.2**).

Julian, *Letter to the Senate and People of Athens* 279D – 280C (V2.1).

Notitia Dignitatum (west) 7 (Z2.3), 11 (Z1.2), 12 (Z1.3), 23 (Z1.1), 28 (Z2.2), 29 (Z2.3), 40 (Z2.1).

Orosius, *History against the Pagans* 7.22.10 (P1), 7.34.9 (X2.2), 7.40.4 (Y2.1).

Orosius was a Spaniard who wrote a history of Rome to AD 417, justifying Christianity against pagan claims that Christianity had brought about the decline of Rome.

Panegyric of Constantine (Pan.Lat. 6) 5.1–4 (**S1.4**), 7.1 (S1.5).

Panegyric of Constantius (Pan.Lat. 8) 11.1 (**S1.1**), 11.2–4 (A13.5), 12–17 (S1.2), 14.2 (K1.3), 19 (S1.3).

Panegyric of Theodosius I (Pan.Lat. 2) 5.1 (**W2.3**).

Panegyrics were speeches usually delivered in honour of an emperor's achievements and in his presence. They thus abound in gross adulation and hyperbole and the names of the authors are mostly (and rightly) forgotten.

Pausanias, *Description of Greece* 8.43.3–4 (**K1.2**).

Pliny (elder), *Natural History* 4.102 (G4), 30.13 (C1.2).

The elder Pliny, who died in the eruption of Vesuvius in AD 79, compiled his *Natural History*, an encyclopaedia of ancient knowledge of the world, from previous writers, adding his own observations.

Plutarch, *Life of Caesar* 23.2–3 (A13.2); *On the Disuse of Oracles* 2 (H2.1), 18 (H2.2).

Plutarch was a Greek politician and scholar of the later 1ˢᵗ and early 2ⁿᵈ century AD, who wrote paired biographies of famous ancient Greek and Roman leaders and various ethical works.

Pomponius Mela, *Geography* 3.49–53 (**E1**).

Procopius, *Vandal War* 1.2.37–38 (**Y4.2**).

Statius, *Silvae* 5.2.53–6 (**G3.1**), 5.2.142–9 (**G3.2**).

Strabo, *Geography* 2.5.8 (**B3.1**); 4.5.1–2 (**B3.2**), 4.5.3 (**A13.1, B4.2**), 4.5.4 (**B3.3**).

Strabo was a Greek historian and geographer whose *Geography* was published under Tiberius. Much of his information on the western areas of the Roman Empire derives from Posidonius, another Greek writer who visited Gaul and Spain in the 90s BC, but Strabo adds occasional comments relevant to his own day.

Suetonius, *Deified Julius* 25.1–2 (**A13.3**), 47 (**A13.4**); *Caligula* 44.2 (**D1**), 46.1 (**D2.1**); *Claudius* 17.1–2 (**E2.1**), 17.2–3 (**E7.1**), 21.6 (**E7.5**), 24.3 (**E7.7**), 25.5 (**E15**); *Nero* 18 (**F1**), 39.1 (**F3.1**); *Vespasian* 4.1–2 (**E6.1**); *Titus* 4.1 (**F5**); *Domitian* 10.3 (**H4**).

Gaius Suetonius Tranquillus followed an equestrian career which culminated as Chief Secretary to the emperor Hadrian. His set of biographies of the emperors from Julius Caesar to Domitian was published around AD 120.

Sulpicius Severus, *Chronicle* 2.41 (**V3**).

Tacitus, *Annals* 2.24 (**C1**); 12.23 (**E7.4**), 12.31 (**E8**), 12.32 (**E9**), 12.33–35 (**E10**), 12.36–38 (**E11**), 12.38–39 (**E12**), 12.40 (**E13–14**); 14.29–30 (**F2**), 14.31 (**F3.2**), 14.32–37 (**F3.4**), 14.38 (**F4.1**), 14.39 (**F4.2**).
Histories 1.2 (**H1.2**), 1.9 (**G1.1**), 1.59–60 (**G1.2**); 2.65 (**G1.3**), 2.66 (**G1.4**); 3.44 (**G1.5**), 3.45 (**G2**).

Cornelius Tacitus was a senator and great orator of the later 1ˢᵗ and early 2ⁿᵈ century AD. After three minor works including the *Agricola*, a memorial of his father-in-law, he wrote two year-by-year histories of recent Rome: the *Histories* (published *c.* 110), covering AD 69 and the Flavians, and the *Annals* (120s?), covering Tiberius to Nero. Much has been lost: the surviving books cover the years AD 14–37, 47–66 and 69–70.

[Tibullus], *Elegies* 3.7.147–50 (**B1**).

Vegetius, *Summary of Military Affairs* 4.37 (**X2.3**).

Verona List 7 (**T2.1**), 13.1 (**T2.2**).

Zosimus, *New History* 1.66.2 (Q1.1), 1.68.1 (Q1.2); 4.35.2-4 (X2.1); 6.2.1–2 (Y2.2), 6.5.2–3 (Y3), 6.10.2 (Y4.1).

Zosimus, probably in the earlier 5th century, wrote (in Greek) a history of the Empire from Augustus until AD 410. For the period 270–404 he drew on his close predecessor Eunapius (see V2.2).

ABBREVIATIONS

HA	Historia Augusta
ILS	H. Dessau, *Inscriptiones Latinae Selectae* [online e-book at Internet Archive: http://www.archive.org/details/inscriptionesla01dessgoog]
L4	LACTOR 4: The Inscriptions of Roman Britain (4th edition)
L19	LACTOR 19: Tiberius to Nero
Mansi II	J.D. Mansi, *Sacrorum Conciliorum Nova Amplissima Collectio*

GLOSSARY

alae: auxiliary cavalry units. From Flavian times, each unit was around 800–1,000 strong.

'**Augustus**': name taken by all emperors; eventually, from the time of Diocletian, the title of the 'senior emperor'. Also title given to many military units and towns (like 'Royal' in UK).

auxiliaries: literally 'helpers' of the regular legions – so archers, cavalry, scouts. Drawn from non-Roman citizens they might eventually achieve citizenship as a reward for their service.

'**Caesar**': title widely applied to emperors; eventually, from the time of Diocletian, the title of the 'junior emperor' (see **R1.1**).

cohort: a unit in the army, usually around 500-strong.

colony (*colonia*): a settlement of veterans (former legionaries) in conquered territory (**E9**).

consul: in the republic, the highest political office; maintained under the emperors as an honour for senior senators.

Count (*comes*): in the late empire, a title of a senior official or general.

denarius: small silver coin. Annual pay for a legionary was 225 denarii per year, increased to 300 by Domitian.

eagle (*aquila*): the military standard of a legion, sacred symbol of the legion itself and carried into battle by the eagle-bearer (*aquilifer*) – see **A2**.

equestrians: members of a class in Roman society almost equal to the senatorial class.

freedman: an ex-slave, formally released by his master. Imperial freedmen (i.e. the emperor's former slaves) could be given positions of great responsibility and power, especially under the Julio-Claudian emperors.

governor: general term for Roman ruler of a province. In Britain, the governor (technically *legatus Augusti pro praetore* – 'representative of the emperor in place of a praetor') was a man of senior status, a former consul, of military and administrative experience, who governed for around 3 years.

kings: often used in the sense of 'friendly kings' – local rulers allowed to keep title and powers while becoming dependent on Rome. On the death of a friendly king, his territory would often pass directly to Rome.

legate: anyone to whom authority had been delegated, *e.g.* a military officer, especially 'legionary legate' the commander of a Roman legion.

legion: the main, infantry, fighting unit of the Roman army, around 5,000 strong.

military tribune: one of six officers in a Roman legion subordinate to the legionary legate (commander).

oppidum (plural: *oppida*): the word is used most basically to describe an urban settlement (**E6.1**); also applied to settlements of some status in provinces, as administrative centres and/or places with numbers of Roman citizens.

ovation: a lesser form of triumph (see below) awarded to victorious generals outside the imperial family.

praetorian cohorts (also 'praetorian guard' or 'the praetorians'): élite soldiers of the Roman army, and the emperor's bodyguard. They numbered 10,000 from Domitian: a detachment would accompany an emperor on campaign.

praetorian prefect: commander of the praetorians, a position of very considerable power.

princeps: the term, meaning 'leader' or 'chief' chosen by Augustus to designate his position. Hence writers of the Julio-Claudian period refer to the 'principate'.

procurator: a direct representative of the emperor.

propraetor: one of the terms for the governor of Britain.

purple: used as a metaphor for imperial rule, so 'presented with the purple robe' means 'made emperor'.

senate: traditionally the ruling council of Rome, maintained by the emperors. Consuls, governors of many provinces including Britain, and new emperors (until the 3rd century) come from the ranks of senators.

quaestor: a junior senator, often gaining experience from assisting a senior senator.

suppliant: someone putting themselves entirely at the mercy of a more powerful man.

triumph: a huge and extravagant military procession to celebrate a victory in battle. From Augustus only members of the imperial family were allowed to triumph, other generals being given 'triumphal ornaments' or an ovation.

veterans: legionary soldiers who had served 25 years in the army. They then 'retired', often to a colony where they would maintain a Roman presence (see **F3.2**).

Vicar (*vicarius*): a deputy; in late empire, a governor-general of a group of provinces (see **V1**).

FROM CAESAR TO CLAUDIUS,
55 BC – AD 41

A.   JULIUS CAESAR

A1.   Caesar decides to mount an expedition to Britain and attempts to discover something about the island beforehand (55 BC)

[4.20.1] Only a little of the summer remained; as the whole of Gaul tends northwards, winter comes early in these regions. Despite this, Caesar made haste to travel to Britain, as he was aware that in almost all of the Gallic Wars, our enemy had received assistance from there [*Book 2.14 – the leaders of the Bellovaci flee to Britain; Book 3.9 – the Veneti send to Britain for reinforcements*]. [20.2] Even if there was not enough time to mount a full campaign, he thought it would still be of great benefit just to go to the island to observe and gain some understanding of the nature of its people, places, ports and approaches, all of which were largely unknown to the Gauls. [20.3] No one has reason to go there except traders, and they themselves know only the coast and areas opposite Gaul. [20.4] Therefore, although he called to him merchants from everywhere, he was unable to learn anything about the size of the island or its tribes, or their warfare practices, or their habits, or which ports would be suitable for many large ships.

[21.1] To discover these things before hazarding his expedition, he identified Gaius Volusenus as the appropriate man to send ahead with a warship, [21.2] and ordered him to explore all these issues and return promptly. [21.3] Caesar himself departed with his entire force for the land of the Morini, from where his crossing to Britain would be the shortest. [21.4] He summoned his ships here from neighbouring areas, and also the fleet which he had created the previous summer for his campaign against the Veneti. [21.5] By this time his intent was known and had been reported to the Britons by merchants; envoys came from several of the island's states, offering hostages and obedience to Roman rule. [21.6] On hearing this, he made them liberal promises and encouraged them to remain loyal, [21.7] then sent them home with Commius, whom he had made king of the Atrebates after conquering them. Caesar approved his virtue and counsel and considered him trustworthy, and his authority in these regions was great. [21.8] He ordered Commius to go to the states he could and encourage them to submit to Rome, and also to announce Caesar's own imminent visit. [21.9] Volusenus viewed all the regions to the extent possible given that he did not dare to leave his ship and entrust himself to the barbarians, and returned to Caesar on the fifth day to report his findings.

[22.1] While Caesar remained where he was to prepare his ships, envoys from a great part of the Morini came to him to apologise for their prior actions, when their barbarism and ignorance of our customs caused them to wage war against Rome, and to assure him that they would do his bidding. [22.2] Caesar considered this approach very opportune because he did not wish to leave enemies at his rear, nor did the time of year facilitate a campaign; and he did not think that these minor issues should take precedence over his occupation of Britain. He demanded a large number of hostages and accepted them under his protection when they were brought to him. [22.3] When about eighty ships had been gathered and brought together, sufficient in his opinion to transport two legions, he shared them, and the warships he had besides, amongst his quaestors, legates and prefects. [22.4] An additional eighteen ships, held eight miles from the port by wind and unable to dock, he gave to the cavalry. [22.5] The rest of the army he gave to Quintus Titurius Sabinus and Lucius Aurunculeius Cotta, his legates, to lead against the Menapii and those cantons of the Morini from which no envoys had come. [22.6] He also ordered his legate Publius Sulpicius Rufus to hold the port with such a garrison as he thought sufficient.

[Caesar, *Gallic Wars* 4.20.1 – 4.22.6]

The Atrebates were a tribe with branches in northern Gaul and southern Britain; compare **A16** on migration. For Commius (also in **A2**, **A4** and **A10**) see further **A14**.

A2. Caesar sets sail from Gaul, reaches Britain and is immediately attacked by the Britons; he defeats the initial attack and the Britons sue for peace

[4.23.1] After making these arrangements, favourable weather allowed Caesar to set sail about the third watch [*midnight – 3 a.m.*], and he ordered the cavalry to head for a farther port, board their ships and follow him. [23.2] They were somewhat tardy in their observance; he himself reached Britain with the first ships around the fourth hour [*10 – 11 a.m.*] and saw the armed enemy forces exposed on the cliffs. [23.3] The nature of this area was such, and the sea so hemmed in by the steep cliffs, that a weapon could be cast from higher ground to the shore. [23.4] Considering this to be an utterly unfit location for debarking, he waited at anchor until the ninth hour [*3 – 4 p.m.*] for the rest of the ships to convene. In the meantime he called together the legates and military tribunes to pass on what he had understood from Volusenus and to make known what he wished them to do; and he warned them that, in line with military principles and especially maritime matters, where events could move rapidly and unpredictably, [23.5] they should carry out his orders at his nod and with precise timing. At the same time as he dismissed them the wind and tide turned, and after giving the signal and raising the anchor he proceeded about seven miles from there and landed his ships on a flat and open shore.

[24.1] But the barbarians, realising the Romans' intentions, sent forward their cavalry and war-chariots, which force they habitually use in battle, and following quickly with the rest of their troops tried to prevent disembarkation from our ships. [24.2] This caused the greatest difficulty because the size of the ships meant that they had to ride in deep water and the soldiers, ignorant of the locale, with their hands encumbered, and burdened with the heavy and weighty load of their weaponry, had to jump down from the ships, keep their footing in the waves and fight the enemy at the same time. [24.3] But the enemy, on dry land or advancing just a little way into the water, with all their limbs free and knowing the terrain very well, boldly threw their weapons or charged their horses, which were accustomed to this. [24.4] Our men were terrified by these things, and lacking any experience with such fighting tactics did not exert the same vim and vigour as they would usually demonstrate in battles on land.

[25.1] When Caesar realised this, he ordered the warships, the appearance of which was somewhat strange to the barbarians and which could move more readily as needed, to move away a little from the transport vessels and to row at speed and draw up on the enemy's exposed flank, and thence drive back and repel the enemy with slings, arrows and artillery; this strategy was of great benefit to our men. [25.2] The shape of the ships, the motion of the oars and the unfamiliar artillery greatly alarmed the barbarians, who paused and retreated, though only a little way. [25.3] Then, while our men hesitated, mostly because of the depth of the sea, the eagle-bearer of the Tenth Legion, after invoking the gods that his actions should turn out well for the legion, called: "Jump down, soldiers, unless you wish to yield the eagle to the enemy! I shall certainly carry out my duty to the state and my leader." [25.4] He said this in a loud voice, threw himself from the ship and bore the eagle towards the enemy. [25.5] Then our men, encouraging each other that such a great disgrace not be incurred, jumped from the ship all together. [25.6] Those from the nearest ships saw them, quickly followed them, and closed with the enemy.

[26.1] Both sides fought vigorously. However our men, who were unable to keep their formation, or get a firm footing, or follow their own standards – men from any ship assembled around whichever standard they came upon – were thrown into great confusion; [26.2] but the enemy, knowing all the shallows, saw from the shore our men leaving their ships one by one, urged on their horses and attacked them while they were hindered; [26.3] many surrounded a few, and others threw their weapons into groups from the exposed side. [26.4] When Caesar observed this he ordered the boats of the warships and also the scouting vessels to be filled with soldiers and sent to assist those he had seen struggling. [26.5] As soon as our men stood on dry land they all charged with all their comrades following and put the enemy to flight; but they were unable to follow far, because the cavalry had not been able to hold course and reach the island. This one thing derailed Caesar's usual success.

[27.1] The enemy, vanquished in battle, sent peace envoys to Caesar immediately they had recovered from their flight, promising to give hostages and render obedience to him. [27.2] With these envoys came Commius of the Atrebates who, as previously mentioned, had been sent ahead to Britain by Caesar. [27.3] When he had disembarked from his ship to fulfil his commission as Caesar's envoy to them, they had seized him and thrown him into chains; they then sent him back after the battle and, [27.4] seeking peace, placed the blame for their actions on the masses and sought forgiveness because of their ignorance. [27.5] Caesar complained that although they themselves had sought peace by sending envoys to him on the Continent, they had initiated war without cause; however, he said he would forgive their ignorance and demanded hostages. [27.6] Some of these they gave immediately, and some they said they would summon from farther regions and hand over in a few days. [27.7] In the meantime they ordered their own people to return to their fields, and the leaders began to come together from all sides to commend themselves and their states to Caesar.

[Caesar, *Gallic Wars* 4.23.1 – 4.27.7]

A3.   The Roman cavalry fail to reach Britain and many of Caesar's ships are damaged by storms; the Britons attack again, and Caesar rescues the Seventh Legion

[4.28.1] By these means, peace was established. Four days after Caesar's arrival in Britain, the eighteen ships previously mentioned as carrying the cavalry set sail with a light wind from their more northerly port. [28.2] When they were nearing Britain and were visible from the camp, such a storm suddenly burst over them that none of them could maintain their course; some of them were blown back to the port from which they had departed, but others were cast to the lower westerly part of the island in great danger. [28.3] However, after dropping anchor they were filling with waves and so, forced to set out on the high seas into the unfavourable night, sought the Continent.

[29.1] That same night the moon happened to be full, which day tends to find the ocean tides at their highest; this circumstance was unknown to our men. [29.2] Thus at one and the same time the tide was filling the warships, with which Caesar had conveyed his army and which he had had drawn up on dry land, and the storm was buffeting the transports, which were riding at anchor; there was no way for our men to minister to them or help. [29.3] A great many ships were wrecked and the others were left unfit to sail because they lost their cables, anchors and rigging. As one might expect would happen, this thoroughly distressed the army. [29.4] There were no other ships which could carry them back, none of the equipment necessary for repairs was available, and, as they had expected to spend the winter in Gaul, no provision of corn had been made for winter here.

[30.1] On realising this, the leaders of the Britons, who had come together at Caesar's camp after the battle, discussed the matter amongst themselves. They were aware that the Romans had no cavalry, ships or corn and knew from the limitations of the camp, which were the more evident because Caesar had transported the legions without baggage, that the army was rather small. [30.2] So they determined that their best course of action was to lead a rebellion in order to interfere with the supply of corn and provisions and draw out the affair until winter, because they were sure that if the Romans were beaten or prevented from returning, no one would cross to Britain intending to make war on them. [30.3] Therefore they entered into conspiracy and left the camp by degrees to begin summoning their people from the fields.

[31.1] But the fate of his ships and the fact that the giving of hostages was interrupted caused Caesar, though not yet aware of their intentions, to suspect that this very thing might happen. [31.2] Therefore he prepared contingency plans for all possible cases. He had corn brought from the field every day and used wood and bronze from the most seriously damaged ships to repair the rest; he ordered that the equipment required for this should be brought from the Continent. [31.3] These issues were dealt with by the soldiers with the greatest zeal; twelve ships were lost, but the rest were made ready to be sailed.

[32.1] While these things were ongoing one legion, which was called the Seventh, had been sent for corn as usual. At that time no suspicion of war had arisen, as some of the native men were still in the fields and some even came often to the camp. Then those who were stationed in front of the camp gates reported to Caesar that they could see a greater quantity of dust than usual in the area to which the legion had marched. [32.2] Caesar, suspecting what it was, that the barbarians had initiated a new plan, ordered the cohorts on duty to set out for that area with him, two other cohorts to replace them at their posts, and the rest to arm themselves and follow him promptly. [32.3] When just a short way from the camp he realised that his men were closely pressed and barely holding their line, and that the legion was closely engaged, with weapons being thrown from all around. [32.4] Because one part remained after all the corn had been harvested from the rest of the fields, the enemy thought it likely that our men would come there and so hid themselves in the woods at night. [32.5] They then attacked suddenly when our men were dispersed and had laid down their arms while busy with the harvest; they killed a few and threw the rest into complete confusion and uncertain order, and at the same time surrounded them with cavalry and chariots.

[Caesar, *Gallic Wars* 4.28.1 – 4.32.5]

A4.   Chariot warfare; the Britons plan to attack once more and are defeated; Caesar agrees peace terms and returns to Gaul

[4.33.1] This is how they fight with chariots. First they ride around on all sides and hurl weapons, and by the very dread of the horses and clattering of the wheels they throw a large part of the ranks into confusion; and when they have penetrated the cavalry troops, they jump down from the chariots and engage on foot. [33.2] Meanwhile the charioteers withdraw from the battle little by little and then arrange their chariots so that if their men are closely pursued by the enemy horde, they have a means of retreat available to them. [33.3] So they display in battle the mobility of cavalry and the stability of infantry, and through intense daily use and practice are so well-trained that they are accustomed to hold back their galloping horses on a precipitous slope, to control and turn them in a short time, and to run along the pole, stand on the yoke and then very quickly regain the chariot.

[34.1] Although our men had been thrown into confusion by these new tactics, Caesar brought help at the most opportune moment; for at his arrival the enemy paused, and our men recovered from their fear. [34.2] After this he considered that it was the wrong time to initiate and commit to battle, so he held his own position and after a short time led his legions back to the camp. [34.3] While these things were happening and all our men were occupied, those Britons who were left in the fields departed. [34.4] For several consecutive days there were storms, which kept our men in the camp and prevented the enemy from fighting. [34.5] In the meantime the barbarians despatched messengers to all areas and made it known that our army was few in number, and explained what a great opportunity would present itself for getting booty and freeing themselves for ever, if they could drive the Romans out of their camp. [34.6] In this way they very quickly gathered a great multitude of infantry and cavalry, and set out for the camp.

[35.1] Caesar saw that the outcome would be the same as on the previous days, that if the enemy were routed they would quickly escape danger. Nonetheless, since he had obtained around thirty cavalry brought over by Commius the Atrebatan, who has been mentioned previously, he arranged the legions in a line in front of the camp. [35.2] When battle commenced the enemy, unable to withstand our soldiers' charge for long, turned and fled. [35.3] Our men followed them for as great a distance as their speed and strength permitted and slew quite a few of them, then returned to the camp after setting fire to all buildings far and wide.

[36.1] That same day envoys were sent by the enemy to Caesar, seeking peace. [36.2] Caesar doubled the number of hostages which he had previously demanded from them, and he ordered that they be brought to the Continent, because the equinox was approaching and he did not deem it wise to subject his weakened ships to a winter sailing. [36.3] He himself, favoured by suitable weather, set sail a little after midnight, and all the ships came safely to the Continent. [36.4] However two transports were not able to reach the same port as the others and were carried down to one a little lower.

[37.1] When approximately three hundred men had disembarked from these ships and were hastening to the camp, the Morini, whom Caesar had left pacified on setting out for Britain, drawn by the hope of booty, surrounded them initially in no great numbers of their own, and ordered them to lay down their arms if they did not wish to be killed. [37.2] Our men formed a circle to defend themselves, and at the loud shouting, another six thousand or so men of the Morini came quickly. When told of this, Caesar sent all of the cavalry from the camp to his men's assistance. [37.3] Meanwhile our soldiers resisted the enemy's charge and for more than four hours fought very bravely; they suffered few wounds but killed many of the enemy. [37.4] But after our cavalry came into view, the enemy threw away their arms and fled, and a great number of them were killed.

[38.1] The next day Caesar sent his legate Titus Labienus, with the legions which he had brought back from Britain, against the Morini, who had revolted. [38.2] The Morini did not have anywhere to retreat to because the swamps which they had used for refuge the year before were dry, so almost all of them handed themselves over to Labienus. [38.3] The legates Quintus Titurius and Lucius Cotta, who had led legions into the territory of the Menapii, came back to Caesar after they had ravaged all the fields, cut down the corn and burnt the buildings, because all of the Menapii had hidden themselves in their thickest woods. [38.4] Caesar set up winter quarters for all the legions in the Belgic lands. Just two of the British states sent hostages to him; the rest neglected to do so. [38.5] After all of this, as a result of Caesar's dispatches, a twenty-day thanksgiving was decreed by the Senate.

[Caesar, *Gallic Wars* 4.33.1 – 4.38.5]

A 'thanksgiving' (*supplicatio*) was decreed by the Senate to avert calamity or give thanks for a great victory. The statues of the gods were placed on couches in front of their temples to receive offerings of wine and incense from all citizens, male and female. It was now subject to competitive inflation: a 10-day thanksgiving had been decreed in 63 BC for Pompey's eastern victory against Mithridates, and a 15-day thanksgiving in 56 BC for Caesar's conquest of Gaul.

A5.   Caesar prepares for a second expedition to Britain (54 BC)

[5.1.1] When Lucius Domitius and Appius Claudius were consuls [*54 BC*], Caesar, about to leave his winter quarters for Italy, as he was wont to do every year, ordered the legates who commanded the legions to build as many ships as they could during the winter, and to repair the old ones. He showed them the style and shape of these. [1.2] For loading expeditiously and hauling up on land he made them a little lower than those which we tend to use on our sea – this the more so since he had discovered that because of the frequent changes of the tides, the waves there were less great; for transporting freight and a great number of beasts of burden he made them slightly wider than those we use on other seas. [1.3] He ordered all of them to be built for speed in regard to which issue their lowness helped very much. [1.4] He commanded that the materials needed for arming the ships be brought from Spain. [1.5] He himself set out for Illyricum when the court sessions for Hither Gaul had ended... *(to settle the Pirustae, who were raiding communities across the frontier).*

[2.1] When these matters had been brought about and the court sessions had ended, he returned to Hither Gaul and from there set out for the army. [2.2] When he arrived there and went around all the winter quarters, he found that by the singular exertion of the soldiers in the face of the greatest scarcity of all resources, about six hundred ships of the type we described above and twenty-eight warships had been built; and they were not far from being ready to launch in just a few days. [2.3] After praising very highly the soldiers and those who had commanded the labour, he disclosed what he wanted done and ordered all to assemble at Port Itius [*Boulogne*], from which port he had discovered the crossing to Britain was the most convenient, about a thirty-mile passage from the Continent; he left what he considered to be enough soldiers for this task...

(Caesar then went with four legions to the land of the Treveri, whose rival leaders Cingetorix and Indutiomarus subsequently submitted – Cingetorix willingly and enthusiastically, Indutiomarus reluctantly and resentfully).

[5.1] After these matters had been decided, Caesar arrived at Port Itius with the legions. [5.2] There he learnt that sixty ships, which had been built in the territory of the Meldi, had been driven back by a storm and, unable to hold their course, had returned to their place of departure; he found the rest prepared to sail and equipped in all respects. [5.3] At the same place gathered many cavalry from Gaul, four thousand in number, and leaders from all the states. [5.4] Out of these he had decided to leave in Gaul a very few, whose loyalty to himself he had observed, and to bring the rest with him in place of hostages; because he was afraid of a Gallic revolt while he was away... *(Caesar planned to take several anti-Roman leading Gauls to Britain to prevent them fomenting rebellion; Dumnorix the Aeduan refused to go)...* [7.3] And so, since he was delayed in that place for around twenty-five days, because the north-west wind, which usually blew in these regions for the greater part of every season, prevented sailing, Caesar focussed on means of trying to contain Dumnorix, while equally discovering his plans. [7.4] At last he got appropriate weather and ordered the soldiers and cavalry to embark… *(Dumnorix fled the camp, pursued by Roman cavalry, and was killed).*

[Caesar, *Gallic Wars* 5.1.1 – 5.7.4]

A6. Caesar, leaving Labienus in charge in Gaul, sets sail and lands unopposed; subsequently he engages and routs the enemy

[5.8.2] Caesar himself, with five legions and the same number of cavalry as he had left on the Continent, set sail at sunset, carried forth on a gentle south-westerly wind. Around midnight the wind dropped so he could not hold course, and he was borne far by the tide; at first light he saw Britain at some distance to port. [8.3] Then following afresh the turning tide, he strove by oar to reach that part of the island which he knew, from the previous summer, was the best for disembarkation. [8.4] In this situation the valour of the soldiers was most praiseworthy; rowing non-stop, they kept the heavy transports level with the warships. [8.5] Around noon the entire fleet reached Britain, but the enemy could not be sighted at that place. [8.6] In fact, as Caesar later discovered from his captives, they had convened there in great strength. However, terrified by the multitude of ships, more than eight hundred of which were seen at one time, including last year's and private ones which some had built for their convenience, they had decamped from the shore and hidden themselves at a higher location.

[9.1] After the army had disembarked and chosen a suitable location for the camp, Caesar found out from prisoners where the enemy forces had settled. Leaving ten cohorts and three hundred cavalry by the sea to protect the ships, at third watch [*midnight – 3 a.m.*] he marched towards the enemy, fearing less for the ships because he had left them tied up at anchor on a soft-sanded open shore; he appointed Quintus Atrius to the command of the ships' guard. [9.2] He himself advanced about twelve miles during the night and sighted the enemy forces. [9.3] The enemy advanced their cavalry and chariots to the river [*Great Stour, Kent*] from their higher position and began to ward off and fight our men. [9.4] Repulsed by our cavalry, they hid themselves in the woods, a place admirably fortified by nature and by workmanship, which they appeared to have prepared beforehand in the event of a civil war; for all the entrances were blocked by numerous felled trees. [9.5] They themselves rushed out of the woods to fight in loose order, and were preventing our men from entering into the fortifications; [9.6] but the soldiers of the Seventh Legion, forming a 'tortoise' and hurling a rampart against the fortifications, captured the place and drove the enemy from the woods, with our men receiving just a few wounds. [9.7] However Caesar forbade them to pursue those fleeing too far, both because he had no knowledge of the nature of the area, and because a great part of the day had passed and he wished to leave time for the fortification of the camp.

[Caesar, *Gallic Wars* 5.8.1 – 5.9.7]

A7. Caesar's ships are again damaged by a storm; Cassivellaunus becomes commander of the British tribal forces

[5.10.1] The next morning he divided the soldiers and cavalry into three and sent them on an expedition to pursue those who had fled. [10.2] After they had advanced some way, when the last of the fugitives were in sight, cavalry came from Quintus Atrius to Caesar and announced that a very great storm had arisen on the night before and that almost all the ships had been damaged and thrown against the shore, because the anchors and ropes did not hold, and the sailors and steersmen could not endure the force of the storm: [10.3] thus great damage resulted from the collision of the ships.

[11.1] When Caesar learnt these things, he ordered the legions and cavalry to be recalled and to resist attacks en route; he himself returned to the ships. [11.2] He saw personally almost exactly what he had learned from messengers and reports, that around forty ships were lost although the rest seemed repairable with great difficulty. [11.3] So he selected workmen from the legions and ordered others to be summoned from the Continent; [11.4] and he wrote to Labienus that he should build as many ships as he could with the legions he had with him. [11.5] Caesar himself, although the matter was of great effort and labour, decided that it would be most expedient for all the ships to be drawn up and joined with the camp by one fortification. [11.6] He spent about ten days on these matters, and not even at night was the work of the soldiers halted. [11.7] After the ships had been drawn up and the camp very well fortified, he left the same troops as previously as guard for the ships; Caesar himself left for the same place from which he had set out. [11.8] By the time he reached it an even greater force of Britons had assembled there from every quarter, and the chief command and management of the war had been entrusted by common counsel to Cassivellaunus, whose lands were separated from the maritime states by the river known as the Thames, about eighty miles from the sea. [11.9] Before now continual wars had come between this man and the other states; but roused by our arrival, the Britons had set him over the entire war and command.

[Caesar, *Gallic Wars* 5.10.1 – 5.11.9]

A8.   Battle recommences; Caesar crosses the River Thames and invades Cassivellaunus' territory

[5.15.1] The cavalry and chariot-fighters of the enemy joined violently in battle with our cavalry on the march. However our men were superior in all respects and drove them into the woods and hills; [15.2] but pursuing too zealously after killing several, they lost some of their own. [15.3] Some time later, when our men were unaware and busy with the fortification of the camp, the enemy suddenly rushed out of the woods, and after charging those who were stationed on duty forward of the camp, fought fiercely. [15.4] Then two cohorts were sent by Caesar in relief – and these were the first cohorts of the two legions – and they had taken station with a very little distance between themselves when the enemy, since our men were frightened by the new style of fighting, very boldly broke through the middle and withdrew from there safely. [15.5] On that day Quintus Laberius Durus, a military tribune, was killed. After more cohorts had been sent up, the enemy was repulsed.

[16.1] In all this kind of fighting, which on this occasion was fought under the eyes of all and in front of the camp, it was observed that our men, because of the heaviness of their arms, could not pursue those withdrawing or even venture to leave the ranks, being little suited to this kind of enemy. [16.2] Moreover the cavalry engaged in battle with great danger, because the enemy would very often purposely withdraw and separate our men a little from the legions; then they would leap down from their chariots and on foot fight an ill-matched engagement. [16.3] The nature of cavalry battle presented exactly the same danger to our men whether retreating or pursuing. [16.4] This was also the case, that the enemy never fought in close order but here and there, widely spaced; and they had outposts set in different places, so that each followed after the other and the fresh and vigorous relieved the weary.

[17.1] On the following day the enemy stationed themselves on the hills far from the camp and began to show themselves here and there and, more mildly than on the previous day, to challenge our cavalry to combat. [17.2] But at noon, when Caesar had sent three legions and all the cavalry to forage, with the legate Gaius Trebonius, the enemy unexpectedly flew at the foragers from all sides, such that they did not pull back from the standards and legions. [17.3] Charging them fiercely, our men drove them back and did not cease the pursuit until the cavalry, relying for help on the legions they saw behind them, drove the enemy headlong and killing a great number of them, [17.4] did not give them a chance to collect themselves, or make a stand, or jump down from their chariots. [17.5] Immediately after this retreat, the aid which had gathered from every quarter marched away, and after this time, the enemy never fought us with their greatest force.

[18.1] After discovering their intent, Caesar led the army to the River Thames in Cassivellaunus' lands; the river can be crossed on foot in only one place, and this but with difficulty. [18.2] When he arrived there, he observed that on the other bank of the river was marshalled a great enemy force. [18.3] Moreover the bank was fortified by sharp stakes set up before it, and the same kind of stakes were fixed under the water and covered by the river. [18.4] Having learned these facts from captives and deserters, Caesar sent forward the cavalry and ordered the legions to follow immediately. [18.5] But the soldiers went with such speed and fury, with only their heads projecting from the water, that the enemy could not check the charge of the legions and cavalry; they abandoned the banks and committed themselves to flight.

[19.1] When Cassivellaunus, as we have described previously, had set aside all hope of combat, he sent away the greater part of his forces. With the rest, about four thousand chariot-fighters, he watched our progress; he retired a little from the path and hid himself in entangled and wooded places. In the areas where he knew we would march, he forced cattle and people from the fields into the woods, [19.2] and when our cavalry went out into the fields to plunder and ravage more freely, he sent the chariot-fighters from the woods by every path and lane; with great danger to our cavalry he fought them, and through this fear he prevented them from roving more widely. [19.3] This meant that Caesar would not allow anyone to venture any distance from the body of legions; he would harm the enemy as much as the efforts of the legionary soldiers could manage on the way, by ravaging the fields and setting fires.

[Caesar, *Gallic Wars* 5.15.1 – 5.19.3]

A9.   The Trinovantes submit to Caesar, followed by other tribes; Caesar attacks Cassivellaunus' settlement

[5.20.1] The Trinobantes were about the strongest state in those regions. From there young Mandubracius had come to Caesar in continental Gaul, seeking his protection; his father had held sovereignty in that state and had been killed by Cassivellaunus, and he himself had avoided death by fleeing. In the meantime the Trinobantes had sent legates to Caesar and promised to surrender to him and to do his bidding; [20.2] they begged that he defend Mandubracius from Cassivellaunus' wrongdoing and send him to the state, that he might rule and hold sovereignty. [20.3] Caesar ordered from them forty hostages and corn for the army, and sent Mandubracius to them. [20.4] They quickly did as he had ordered, and sent the number of hostages and the corn.

[5.21.1] When he had protected the Trinobantes and prevented wrongdoing by all the soldiers, the Cenimagni, Segontiaci, Ancalites, Bibroci and Cassi sent legates and surrendered to Caesar. [21.2] From them he discovered that not far from that place was Cassivellaunus' town, fortified by woods and marshes, where he had gathered together a satisfactory number of men and cattle. [21.3] However the Britons call a town any entangled woods they have fortified with a rampart and ditch, where they are wont to assemble to avoid enemy incursions. [21.4] Caesar set out for it with the legions; he found it excellently fortified by nature and workmanship; however, he hastened to attack it from two sides. [21.5] The enemy held out for a little while but did not resist the onslaught of our troops, and rushed out from another part of the town. [21.6] There was found a great number of cattle, and many people were caught in flight and killed.

[Caesar, *Gallic Wars* 5.20.1 – 5.21.6]

The name of the tribe now commonly known as the Trinovantes was sometimes written as Trinobantes. It has been suggested that the Cenimagni may be synonymous with the tribe known as the Iceni.

A10.   Cassivellaunus sends to other tribes for help, but is defeated; Caesar returns to Gaul

[5.22.1] While these things were happening in these places, Cassivellaunus sent messages to Kent – which we described previously as being by the sea, and in which regions four kings ruled, Cingetorix, Carvilius, Taximagulus and Segovax – and ordered them to assault and besiege the naval camp unexpectedly after gathering all their forces. [22.2] When they came to the camp, our men sallied forth and killed many of them and also captured the noble leader Lugotorix; then they withdrew uninjured. [22.3] Cassivellaunus was informed of this battle; as he had sustained so many defeats and so much of his lands had been ravaged, and especially influenced by the rebellion of the states, through Commius the Atrebatan he sent ambassadors for surrender to Caesar. [22.4] Since Caesar had decided to spend the winter on the Continent because of the unexpected revolt of the Gauls, and because not much of the summer was left and he realised that it would be easy to drag it out, he requisitioned hostages and decided what taxes Britain should pay each year to the people of Rome. [22.5] He enjoined and ordered Cassivellaunus not to harm Mandubracius or the Trinobantes.

[5.23.1] When he had received the hostages, Caesar led the army back to the sea and found the ships rebuilt. [23.2] After launching them, because he had a great number of captives and because some ships had been destroyed by the storm, he arranged to return the army in two trips. [23.3] And so it happened that out of so great a number of ships and with so many voyages, in neither this nor the previous year was even one ship bearing soldiers lost. [23.4] However, out of those which were sent back to him empty from the Continent, both those which had landed soldiers on the previous expedition and those which Labienus had subsequently arranged to be built, numbering sixty, very few reached their destination and almost all the rest were forced back. [23.5] When Caesar had waited in vain for these for some days, he necessarily quartered the soldiers more closely, so that he should not be prevented from sailing by the time of year as the equinox was approaching. A total calm followed [23.6] and he set sail at the beginning of the second watch [*9 p.m. – midnight*]; at first light he reached land and brought all the ships over safely.

[Caesar, *Gallic Wars* 5.22–23]

A11.   Cicero writes to Atticus about his brother Quintus, who has accompanied Caesar on his second expedition to Britain

A11.1.   My brother Quintus' letter gives one the impression that he is now in Britain. I am anxiously waiting for news of him. *(27 July 54 BC)*

[Cicero, *Letters to Atticus* 4.15.10]

A11.2.   And now for the rest of my news. My brother in his letter gives me almost incredible news of Caesar's affection for me, and this is borne out by a very full letter from Caesar himself. We await the outcome of the war in Britain; it is known that the approaches to the island are "fenced about with daunting cliffs": and it has also become clear that there is not a scrap of silver on the island; there's no prospect of booty except slaves – and I don't imagine you are expecting any knowledge of literature or music among them! *(October 54 BC)*

[Cicero, *Letters to Atticus* 4.16.7]

A11.3.   On 24 October I received letters from my brother Quintus and Caesar; they were addressed on 25 September from the nearest point on the British coast. The campaign in Britain is over; hostages have been taken, and although there's no booty, a tribute has been levied. They are bringing the army back from Britain. *(late October 54 BC)*

[Cicero, *Letters to Atticus* 4.18.5]

Marcus Tullius Cicero, consul in 63 BC, was a political opponent of Caesar's, but they maintained friendly relations and Caesar courted Cicero's support, which is why he had accepted Quintus, Cicero's younger brother, on his staff.

A12.   Cassius Dio's accounts of Caesar's campaigns in Britain

A12.1. [39.50.1] Caesar was then the first Roman to cross the Rhine, and later, when Pompey and Crassus were consuls (*55 BC*), he made the crossing to Britain. [50.2] This country is four hundred and fifty stades distant from the continent at the shortest point where the Morini are, runs alongside the rest of Gaul and almost all of Spain, and extends into the open sea... [50.4] With the passing of time it has been demonstrated clearly to be an island, first under the propraetor Agricola and now under the emperor Severus.

[51.1] Caesar then was eager to cross to this land, now that the rest of Gaul was quiet and he had won over the Morini. He made the crossing at the most suitable point with his infantry but did not land where he should, for the Britons had advance knowledge of his crossing and had secured all the landing places facing the continent. [51.2] So he sailed round a projecting headland and along its other side. He disembarked in the shallows, defeating those who opposed him, and gained dry land before more enemy reinforcements could arrive, and later drove them off too when they attacked. [51.3] Not many of the barbarians fell because they were in chariots or on horses and easily escaped the Romans whose cavalry was still not present. However, alarmed at the reports from the continent about the Romans and at the fact they had actually dared to make the crossing and had effected a landing, they sent some men of the Morini who were their friends to negotiate with Caesar. [52.1] When he asked for hostages, they were at that time willing to give them, but when the Romans then suffered damage from a storm to the fleet that was present and the one on its way, they changed their minds. Although they did not make an open assault, for the Roman camp was strongly defended, [52.2] they lay in wait for some men who had been sent to collect supplies on the assumption that the country was friendly to them and killed them bar a few, for Caesar swiftly came to the rescue of the survivors, and after that they even launched an attack on the Roman fortification. They achieved nothing and came off badly, but they would not make an agreement until after several setbacks. [52.3] Indeed Caesar would have had no intention of making peace with them, except that winter was coming and he was not accompanied by sufficient forces to wage warfare in that season with the setback to the others being brought over, and the Gauls had revolted in response to his absence. So against his will he came to terms with them, and asked for many hostages then, but only received a few.

[53.1] Caesar sailed back to the continent and quelled the uprisings. He had acquired nothing from Britain for himself or the Romans except the fame of having campaigned against them. He prided himself enormously on this, and the Romans at home made an amazingly great fuss about it... [53.2] and voted to celebrate a twenty-day holiday for it.

[Cassius Dio, *Roman History* 39.50.1 – 39.53.2]

For 450 stades (83 km / 52 miles) as the width of the English Channel, compare the 100 stades of Diodorus Siculus (**A15** below).
Circumnavigation of Britain under Agricola: see **H1.1** below for Dio's own account.
Twenty-day holiday (*supplicatio*): see note to **A4** above.

A12.2. [40.1.1] In Gaul among other things under those consuls, Lucius Domitius and Appius Claudius (*54 BC*), Caesar prepared ships in between the Roman fast type and the local freighters, in order to make them as light as possible and resistant to the swell, and which could be drawn up on dry land without damage. [1.2] When the sailing season came, he again made the crossing to Britain. The reason he gave was that they had not sent over all the hostages they had promised, thinking that as he had gone away empty-handed that time, he would not make another attempt against them. In reality, however, he was terribly fixated on the island, so that, if this had not been the case, he would certainly have found some other excuse.

[1.3] He came to land at the same place as before and, since no one dared to oppose him because of the number of his ships and because they approached at several points simultaneously, he immediately gained control of the anchorage. [2.1] Being unable for those reasons to prevent his landing, and in greater fear than before because he had come with a larger army, the barbarians gathered all their most valuable things into the most overgrown and wooded of the nearby places, [2.2] and made them safe by cutting down the surrounding timber and piling other timber in layers on top of it so they were in a sort of stockade. Then they harassed the Roman foraging parties, and after coming off worse in a battle in open ground, they lured the Romans in pursuit there and in turn killed lots of them. [2.3] Subsequently, when a storm again damaged the Roman ships, the Britons summoned allies and set out against the Roman beach-head itself, after making Cassivellaunus, the foremost of the chiefs in the island, their leader. [2.4] In confronting them the Romans were at first thrown into disorder by their chariot charges, but then they opened ranks and launched their weapons at their flanks as they sped fast, and made the battle equal. [3.1] For the time being both sides remained in their positions. When the barbarians again got the better of the infantry but were worsted by the cavalry, they retreated across the Thames and encamped after cutting off the ford with stakes, some visible and some under water, [3.2] However, when Caesar by a fierce assault forced them to abandon the staked crossing and, after that, drove them out of their stockade by a siege, while the other Romans repelled an attack on their anchorage, the Britons took fright and made terms, including giving hostages and imposition of an annual tribute.

[4.1] In these circumstances Caesar departed completely from the island and left no army there, for it would have been risky to winter in a foreign land. Also, thinking that it would not be a good idea to be absent for longer from Gaul, he was satisfied with the situation so as not to lose what he had by stretching out for more. [4.2] It seems that he was right to do so, as was shown by events, for when he reached Italy to spend the winter there, the Gauls, despite the many garrisons in each community, started causing trouble, and even revolted openly. If this had happened while Caesar had remained in Britain for the winter, all Gaul would have been in turmoil.

[Cassius Dio, *Roman History* 40.1.1 – 40.4.1]

A13. Other accounts of Caesar's campaigns in Britain

See also the summary in Tacitus, *Agricola* 13.

A13.1. The deified Caesar crossed over twice to the island, but came back in haste without accomplishing much or proceeding very far inland. This was not only because of trouble in Gaul involving both the barbarians and his own troops, but also because many of his ships were lost at full moon when the tides are at their greatest. However he won two or three victories over the Britons, even though he took over only two legions, and brought back hostages, slaves and much other booty.

[Strabo, *Geography* 4.5.3]

A13.2. [23.2] His campaign against Britain involved remarkable daring. He was the first to bring a fleet to the western Ocean and he sailed across the Atlantic sea with an army to make war. Reports of the island's size had made men doubt its existence, and there was considerable disagreement among many writers who considered that the name and description had been invented and belonged to an island which had never existed and did not now; and in attempting to occupy it Caesar carried the supremacy of Rome beyond the bounds of the civilised world. [3] He sailed twice across to the island from the point of Gaul immediately opposite, and in the course of numerous battles did more harm to the enemy than good to his own men. There was nothing worth taking from the inhabitants, who led mean and poor lives, and Caesar did not bring the war to the sort of conclusion he wanted, although before sailing away from the island again he took hostages from the king and fixed a tribute.

[Plutarch, *Life of Caesar* 23.2–3]

A13.3. [25.1] Briefly this is what he did in the nine years during which he held office. Excepting those tribes which were in alliance with him and had served him well, he reduced to provincial status the whole of that part of Gaul which is bounded by the Pyrenees, the Alps, and the Cevennes, and by the rivers Rhine and Rhone, an area with a circumference of about 3,200 miles; and he imposed on it an annual tribute of 40,000,000 sesterces. [2] He built a bridge across the Rhine and became the first Roman to attack and defeat heavily the Germans on the other side. He also attacked the Britons, a people unknown before, and after defeating them exacted sums of money and took hostages. Among so many successes he only suffered set-backs on three occasions: in Britain when his fleet was almost destroyed by a violent storm; in Gaul when a legion was put to flight at Gergovia; and in German territory when his officers Titurius and Aurunculeius were killed in an ambush.

[Suetonius, *Deified Julius* 25.1–2]

A13.4. They say that his attack on Britain was inspired by the prospect of pearls; sometimes he weighed them in his own hand when he was comparing their size.

[Suetonius, *Deified Julius* 47]

A13.5. [11.2] When (Julius) Caesar, the originator of your name, first of all the Romans entered Britain, he wrote that he had found another world... [3] But at that time Britain was not prepared with ships for any kind of naval contest... [4] In addition to this, the nation of the Britons was still at that time uncivilised and used to fighting only with the Picts and the Hibernians, both still half-naked enemies; and so they submitted to Roman arms so easily that the only thing that Caesar ought to have boasted of was that he had navigated the Ocean.

[*Panegyric of Constantius* 11.2–4]

For this speech, made in AD 297 to honour Constantius I following his defeat of Allectus, see **S1** below.

A14. Commius rebels against Caesar

When Commius the Atrebatan had been defeated by the deified Julius and was fleeing from Gaul to Britain, he happened to reach the sea at a moment when the wind was favourable but the tide was out. In spite of the fact that the ships were stuck on the dry beach he ordered the sails to be spread. Caesar was pursuing him but when he saw in the distance the sails swelling and filled with the wind, he thought Commius was voyaging safely out of reach, and withdrew. *(Late 50s BC)*

[Frontinus, *Stratagems* 2.13.11]

According to Caesar's *Gallic Wars*, Commius remained loyal to Caesar for only a few years, from the conquest of the Atrebates in Gaul in 57 BC until around 53 BC, when Labienus discovered that he was plotting against Caesar with other tribes. Volusenus was sent with a small party to kill him; Commius sustained a severe head wound but survived. In 52 BC he joined an alliance of Gallic tribes to relieve Alesia from Roman siege, and upon that defeat joined the rebellion of the Bellovaci, which also failed. Mark Antony ordered Volusenus to kill him in 51 BC; though Volusenus won the skirmish, Commius escaped. He subsequently sued for peace. It is unclear whether the journey to Britain described above was as a result of this truce breaking down and hostilities being resumed, or whether exile from Gaul was part of the truce agreement. Commius was well established as ruler of the Atrebates in Britain by 30 BC, as attested by coins minted at Calleva Atrebatum (Silchester, Hampshire); coins *L4* 1 and 4 refer to Tincomarus and Verica as sons of Commius.

Sextus Julius Frontinus was a senator of the late 1st century AD who wrote handbooks on various practical subjects. He had himself governed Britain around AD 74–77: see Tacitus, *Agricola* 17.3–4.

A15. Diodorus Siculus' description of Britain

[5.21.1] Facing the ocean coast of Gaul. . . there are many islands in the ocean, the largest of which is called Britain. [21.2] This island was not visited by foreign forces in ancient times; neither Dionysus nor Hercules is recounted to have campaigned against it, nor any other hero or warlord. In our time Gaius Julius Caesar, who was called a god for his achievements, was the first recorded conqueror of the island, for he defeated the Britons and forced them to pay fixed tributes. However we shall describe the events relating to this in detail under the appropriate dates. Here we discuss the island and the tin which it produces.

[21.3] Britain is triangular in shape, very like Sicily, and has sides of unequal length. It stretches out obliquely alongside Europe. They say that the promontory called Cantium [*Kent*], the least distant point from the Continent, is around one hundred stades away at the place where the sea [*North Sea*] makes its outlet. The second headland, the one called Belerium [*Land's End, Cornwall*], is said to be four days' sailing from the Continent, and the remaining one is recorded to extend into the open sea, [21.4] and is called Orca [*Duncansby Head, north-east Scotland*].

The shortest of the sides is seven thousand five hundred stades and extends alongside Europe. The second, from the straits to the peak, is fifteen thousand stades and the last of twenty thousand stades, so that the total circumference of the island is forty-two thousand five hundred stades.

[21.5] They say that Britain is inhabited by indigenous peoples whose behaviour preserves the ancient way of life. For instance they use chariots in their wars, just as the ancient heroes of the Greeks are recounted to have used them in the Trojan War, and they have basic dwellings constructed mostly of reeds or timber. They do the harvesting of their grain crops by cutting off the ears of grain and storing them in their roofed dwellings, from which they select the old ears each day [21.6] and grind them to make food.

Their habits are simple and quite removed from the cleverness and wickedness of men today. Their lifestyle is basic, and they are far separated from the luxury which comes with wealth. The island is also well populated, and the climate has a decidedly cold nature from lying right under the (Great) Bear. There are many kings and warlords, and mostly they exist at peace with one another.

[22.1] However we shall describe in detail their customs and other distinct features when we get to Caesar's expedition to Britain. Here we discuss the tin which it produces. The inhabitants of Britain of the promontory called Belerium are especially open to foreigners and more up-to-date in their behaviour because of interaction with foreign merchants. It is they who produce the tin, working the area that bears it with skilled techniques.

[Diodorus Siculus, 5.21.1 – 5.22.1]

5.22.2–4 describes how the Britons quarried and processed the tin before taking it on wagons to 'Ictis' – often taken to be St Michael's Mount off the coast of Cornwall, but more probably the Isle of Wight, called Vectis in Latin, where it was sold to merchants who then transported it across Gaul to the mouth of the Rhone, i.e. for shipment through the Mediterranean.

An Attic stade, the most common measure of distance in the Hellenistic period, is 185 metres. Diodorus' measurements, taken from Pytheas' circumnavigation of Britain c. 300 BC, give the sides as 1,388 km / 862 miles, 2,775 km / 1,724 miles and 3,700 km / 2,299 miles, making a total of 7,863 km / 4,886 miles – or over twice the actual straight-line length of the combined coastlines. However the narrowest width of the English Channel from Kent to the Continent, which Diodorus gives as 18.5 km / 11.5 miles, is around 33 km / 21 miles. See **N2.2** below on the size of Britain according to Cassius Dio, and **A12.1** above on the distance from the continent.

Diodorus Siculus wrote (in Greek) a universal history down to 60 BC, his own time, so he never reached Caesar's campaigns as he promised in this passage. The first five Books describe the geography of the known world, based mainly on previous Greek writers such as Posidonius, who had toured Gaul and Spain in the 90s BC.

A16. Caesar's description of Britain

[5.12.1] The interior portion of Britain is inhabited by those who claim, on the strength of tradition, to be native to the island, [12.2] and the coastal areas by those who crossed over from Belgium to wage war for booty; almost all of these are called by the names of the states from which they originated and came across. When the war had been concluded they remained there and began to cultivate the fields. [12.3] The number of men is infinite and the buildings close together, just like those of the Gauls, and there are a great many cattle. [12.4] They use either bronze or gold coins, or instead of coins iron rods measured to a fixed weight. Tin is found in the inland regions and iron on the coast, but of this the supply is scanty; they use imported bronze. [12.5] There are the same kinds of timber as in Gaul, except beech and fir. [12.6] They do not think it lawful to eat hare, poultry or goose; they do, however, breed them for amusement and pleasure. [12.7] The climate is more temperate than in Gaul, and the cold milder.

[13.1] The island is triangular in shape, and one side is opposite Gaul. Of this side one angle, which is in Kent, where almost all ships from Gaul land, lies towards the east, and the lower towards the south. This side extends about five hundred miles. [13.2] Another side tends towards Spain and the west; Ireland is off this side, and is estimated to be half the size of Britain, though the passage is as long as from Gaul to Britain. [13.3] In the middle of this voyage is an island, which is called Mona [*Anglesey*]; moreover several smaller islands are reckoned to lie near, about which islands some have written that during winter, it is night for thirty days without interruption. [13.4] We found out nothing about this by enquiry, but with unerring measurements with water-clocks we saw that the nights were shorter than on the Continent. [13.5] The length of this side, as their opinion asserts, is seven hundred miles. [13.6] third side tends north; no land lies opposite, but the angle of that side looks principally towards Germany. This side is reckoned to be eight hundred miles in length. [13.7] Thus the whole island is two thousand miles in circumference.

[14.1] Of all the natives, by far the most civilised are those who inhabit Kent, a region which is entirely coastal, and they do not differ greatly from Gallic custom. [14.2] Most of the inland inhabitants do not sow corn but live on milk and meat and are clad in skins. [14.3] Indeed all the Britons dye themselves with woad, which results in a dark blue colour, and thereby they have a more terrible appearance in battle; they let their hair grow and have every part of the body shaved apart from the head and upper lip. [14.4] Wives are held in common by groups of ten or twelve, especially brothers with brothers and fathers with sons; [14.5] but those born from these wives are held to be the children of those to whom each young woman was first given in marriage.

[Caesar, *Gallic Wars* 5.12.1 – 5.14.5]

A17.   Caesar's account of Gallic society and the Druids

[6.11.2] In Gaul there are rival groups (*factiones*) not only in all tribes (*civitates*) and all cantons (*pagi*) and their subdivisions, but virtually even in individual households, [11.3] and the leaders (*principes*) of these rival groups are those who are thought, in the judgement of the groups, to have supreme authority (*auctoritas*), and to whom the final decision reverts in all matters and discussions. [11.4] This seems to have been instituted in antiquity with the following purpose, that no man of the people (*plebs*) should lack assistance against a more powerful man, for each leader does not allow his people to be coerced or cheated, and if he did, he would have no authority among them. [11.5] The same principle holds at the highest level of Gaul as a whole, for all the tribes are divided into two parties (led by the Aedui and Sequani)...

[13.1] In all Gaul there are only two types of men who are of any account or status. The common people are almost in the position of slaves: they take no initiative and are never consulted. [13.2] Most are crushed by debt or the burden of taxes or exploitation by powerful men, so bind themselves to serve noble men who have the same rights over them as (Roman) masters have over slaves. [13.3] Of these two types, one is the Druids, the other the knights (*equites*).

[13.4] The Druids are involved in divine affairs: they take care of public and private sacrifices and explain religious issues; a great number of young men crowds around them for their learning, and they are greatly honoured among the Gauls. [13.5] For they decide almost all public and private disputes, and if a crime is brought for hearing or there has been a murder, if there is a dispute about an inheritance or boundaries, they give rulings and decide the compensation or penalty. [13.6] If an individual or community does not abide by their ruling, they exclude them from sacrifices. This is the most severe penalty among the Gauls. [13.7] Those so excluded are held to be among the impious and criminal, and everyone avoids them and shrinks from meeting or speaking to them in case, like a disease, they catch a misfortune. If they seek a judicial hearing, it is denied, and no position of honour is shared with them. [13.8] All these Druids have one chief who has supreme authority among them. [13.9] On his death either one who stands out from rest in reputation succeeds him, or if several are equal, they compete for the position of leader by a ballot of Druids or sometimes even with weapons. [13.10] At a fixed time of year they hold council at a sacred site in the territory of the Carnutes, the region which is held to be the centre of all Gaul. Those who have disputes gather here from all sides, and obey the rulings and judgements of the Druids. [13.11] It is thought that their learning was devised in Britain and from there brought across to Gaul, and still now most who wish to study it thoroughly travel there for instruction.

[14.1] The Druids usually avoid war and do not pay such taxes like the rest; they are exempt from military service and free from all other burdens. [14.2] Stimulated by these great advantages, many come for learning of their own accord or are sent by parents and relatives. [14.3] Apparently they learn by heart a great number of texts, and some remain at their learning for 20 years. They do not think it proper to commit these texts to writing, although for almost all other matters, including public and private records, they use Greek letters. [14.4] I think they made this rule for two reasons: because they do not want their learning to be brought to the masses, and because they do not want those who are studying to rely on books and make less effort to remember; for it generally happens that reliance on books reduces diligence and memory in studying seriously. [14.5] Their principal aim is to persuade people that souls do not die but pass from one person to another after death, for they think that abandoning the fear of death is the greatest stimulant to virtue. [14.5] In addition to this they discuss many things – the stars and their motion, the size of the universe and the earth, the nature of the world, the force and powers of the immortal gods – and pass them on to the young.

[15.1] The other type is the 'knights'. When the occasion arises and some war has broken out – which used to happen almost every year before Caesar's arrival, in that they would themselves be launching assaults on others or fending off assaults made on them –they all turn out for war. [15.2] Each of them, in proportion to his ancestry and wealth of resources, surrounds himself with numerous *ambacti* (retainers) and dependants (*clientes*). This is the one way they recognise influence and power.

[16.1] As a nation all the Gauls are addicted to superstitious beliefs, [16.2] and for that reason those afflicted with serious diseases or those engaging in battle or danger sacrifice men in place of animal victims, or promise to sacrifice them, using Druids to carry out these sacrifices. [16.3] They reckon that the divine spirit of the immortal gods can only be placated if for one human life another human life is repaid, and there are established public sacrifices of the same kind. [16.4] Some Gauls make images of immense size whose wickerwork limbs they fill with live men; they are set on fire, and the men lose their lives surrounded by flames. [16.5] They think punishing men guilty of theft, brigandage or some other criminal act is more pleasing to the immortal gods, but when the supply of this sort fails, they resort to punishing the innocent.

[Caesar, *Gallic Wars* 6.11.2 – 6.11.5 and 6.13.1 – 6.16.5]

Caesar's description of Gallic society, which he interprets and expresses mainly in Roman social and political terms, may give some guide to British society of that time. *Ambactus*, the one Gallic term he cites, seems to mean a tied follower or servant, whereas 'clients' to a Roman meant people with obligations but of independent status.

Druids: the main other ancient account is Strabo, *Geography* 4.4.4–5, based on the (lost) earlier account of Posidonius, who emphasised their 'philosophy'. Caesar's claim that Druidism was based in Britain may be part of his excuse for invading (but see also **C1.2** below). All ancient accounts state that the Druids practised human sacrifice (see **F2** below), but Caesar is the only one to mention the 'wicker man' ritual.

B.   AUGUSTUS (31 BC – AD 14)

B1.   Britain remains unconquered

Wherever earth is bounded by Ocean, no part of it, Messalla, will raise arms against you. For you is left the Briton, whom Roman arms have not yet vanquished, and for you the other part of the world with the sun's path between.

[[Tibullus], *Elegies* 3.7.147–150]

This anonymous poem praises the Balkan victories in 35–34 BC of Marcus Valerius Messalla Corvinus, a supporter of Augustus. Messalla was the patron of Tibullus and other poets whose works are preserved as Book 3 of 'Tibullus'.

B2.   Augustus plans to campaign against the Britons

B2.1.   Augustus was also pressing ahead with a British expedition in emulation of his father; after the winter in which Antony for the second time and Lucius Libo held the consulship, he had already reached Gaul when some newly conquered tribes rose in rebellion and were joined by the Dalmatians. *(34 BC)*

[Cassius Dio, *Roman History* 49.38.2]

B2.2.   Augustus also set out to campaign in Britain, but when he came to Gaul he lingered there. The Britons seemed likely to make terms, and affairs in Gaul were still unsettled, since the conquest of the country had been immediately followed by the civil war. *(27 BC)*

[Cassius Dio, *Roman History* 53.22.5]

B2.3.   Augustus was intending to campaign in Britain, where the people would not come to terms, but he was prevented because the Salassi were in revolt and the Cantabri and Astures had been antagonised. *(26 BC)*

[Cassius Dio, *Roman History* 53.25.2]

B2.4.   I pray that you may protect Caesar on his expedition against the Britons, the furthest nation of the world. *(c. 26 BC)*

[Horace, *Odes* 1.35.29–30]

B2.5.   When Jupiter thunders in heaven we know he is king there; and Augustus will be recognised as a god upon earth when he has added the Britons and the menacing Persians to the empire. *(c. 23 BC)*

[Horace, *Odes* 3.5.1–4]

Horace (Quintus Horatius Flaccus) was a lyric poet of the Augustan period, under the patronage of Augustus' friend and adviser Maecenas.
Additional references to Augustus' planned invasions of Britain are Propertius, *Elegies* 2.27.5 and Horace, *Odes* 1.21.13 (earlier 20s BC); there is no mention in Augustan literature after 23 BC of any intent or desire to invade Britain. See Strabo's comments in **B3.1** and **B4.2** below.

B3.   Strabo's description of Britain and Ireland

B3.1.   And for the purposes of political power, there would be no advantage in knowing such (distant) countries and their inhabitants, particularly where the people live in islands which are such that they can neither injure nor benefit us in any way, because of their isolation. For although the Romans could have possessed Britain, they scorned to do so, for they saw that there was nothing at all to fear from Britain, since they are not strong enough to cross over and attack us. No corresponding advantages would arise by taking over and holding the country. For at present more seems to accrue from the customs duties on their commerce than direct taxation could supply, if we deduct the cost of maintaining an army to garrison the island and collect the tribute. The unprofitability of an occupation would be still more marked in the case of the other islands near Britain.

[Strabo, *Geography* 2.5.8]

B3.2.   [4.5.1] Britain is triangular in shape. Its longest side lies parallel to Gaul, and neither exceeds nor falls short of it in length. Each measures about 4,300 or 4,400 stadia [*c*. 800 km or 500 miles] ... (The British shore) extends from Cantion [*Kent*] which is directly opposite the mouth of the Rhine, as far as the westerly end of the island which lies opposite Aquitania and the Pyrenees ...

[4.5.2] There are four crossings in common use from the mainland to the island, those which start from the mouths of rivers – the Rhine, the Seine, the Loire and the Garonne. Those who cross from the Rhineland do not start from the river estuary, but from the territory of the Morini, who border on the Menapii, where Iction lies, which the deified Caesar used as a naval base when he crossed to the island ... Most of the island is low-lying and wooded, but there are many hilly areas. It produces corn, cattle, gold, silver and iron. These things are exported along with hides, slaves and dogs suitable for hunting. The Gauls however use both these and their own native dogs for warfare also.

The men of Britain are taller than the Gauls and not so yellow-haired. Their bodies are more loosely built. This will give you an idea of their size: I myself in Rome saw youths standing half a foot taller than the tallest in the city although they were bandy-legged and ungainly in build. They live much like the Gauls but some of their customs are more primitive and barbarous. Thus for example some of them are well supplied with milk but do not know how to make cheese; they know nothing of planting crops or of farming in general. They are ruled by their own kings. For the most part they use chariots in war, like some of the Gauls. Their cities are the forests, for they fell trees and fence in large circular enclosures in which they build huts and pen in their cattle, but not for any great length of time. The weather tends to rain rather than snow. Mist is very common, so that for whole days at a stretch the sun is seen only for three or four hours around midday. This is the case also among the Morini, the Menapii and the neighbouring peoples.

[Strabo, *Geography* 4.5.1–2]

B3.3. Besides some small islands around Britain, there is another large island, Ierne [*Ireland*], which stretches to the north parallel with Britain, its breadth being greater than its length. About this island I have nothing certain to tell, except that its inhabitants are more savage than the Britons. They are heavy eaters as well as being cannibals. They count it an honourable practice to eat their fathers when they die. They have intercourse with their mothers and sisters as well as other women – but I say this only on the understanding that I can produce no witnesses. The Scythians are also said to be man-eaters, and, when reduced to necessity under siege, the Gauls, the Iberians and several other peoples.

[Strabo, *Geography* 4.5.4]

B4.   Relations with Britain

B4.1.   There fled to me as suppliants various kings: from the Parthians Tiridates and later Phraates son of King Phraates; Artavasdes king of the Medes and Artaxares king of the Adiabeni; from the Britons Dumnobellaunus and Tincomarus.

[Augustus, *Res Gestae* 32.1]

Dumnobellaunus (or Dubnovellaunus) is the name of a king of the Cantiaci in Kent and a king of the Trinovantes in Essex/Suffolk, probably the same person. The name is attested on numerous coins found mostly in Kent, East Anglia and Essex. Dumnobellaunus was driven from Trinovantian territory by Cunobelinus of the Catuvellauni in the late 1st century BC. Tincomarus was a son of Commius and ruler of the Atrebates, whose capital was at Silchester (Calleva Atrebatum) in Hampshire. Several of his coins survive, such as the gold coin *L4* 1.

The *Res Gestae* is Augustus' own summary of his achievements, published after his death in AD 14.

B4.2.   At present however some of the kings have gained the friendship of Caesar Augustus by sending embassies and paying him deference. They have not only dedicated offerings in the Capitol but have also more or less brought the whole island under Roman control. Furthermore they submit to heavy duties on exports to Gaul and on imports from there, which include ivory bracelets and necklaces, amber and glassware and similar petty trifles, so that there is no need of a garrison for the island. It would require at least one legion and a force of cavalry to collect tribute from them, and the cost of such a force would offset the revenue gained. If tribute were imposed the customs duties would inevitably dwindle and at the same time the risks would be greater if force were employed.

[Strabo, *Geography* 4.5.3]

C.   TIBERIUS (AD 14–37)

C1.1.   (After the storm which scattered Germanicus' ships) some were swept over to Britain, and were sent back by the kings of that country. *(AD 16)*

[Tacitus, *Annals* 2.24]

There are no other mentions of Britain in the sources for Tiberius. Germanicus, Tiberius' adopted son, was campaigning in the area of the River Ems.

C1.2.   Magic had a hold on both provinces of Gaul, indeed right down to our own times. For the principate of Tiberius Caesar did away with their Druids and the whole tribe of prophets and healers. But . . . still today awestruck Britain practises magic with such grand rituals that it might seem she gave it to the Persians [*i.e. magi*].

[Pliny, *Natural History* 30.13]

D.   GAIUS (CALIGULA) (AD 37–41)

D1.   Adminius' surrender

Gaius did nothing more than to receive the surrender of Adminius, son of Cunobellinus king of the Britons, who had been exiled by his father and had fled to the Romans with a small force. But, as if the whole island had surrendered to him, he sent exaggerated letters to Rome, ordering the messengers to drive their vehicles right into the Forum and up to the Senate House, and only to deliver the letters to the consuls before a full meeting of the Senate in the temple of Mars.

[Suetonius, *Caligula* 44.2]

There are coins of Amminus/Amminius which prove the existence of a British ruler of this name in eastern Kent in the earlier 1st century AD, before his exile. Cunobelinus is also attested in coinage – see *L4* 5 and 6.

D2. Caligula's attempt to mount a British campaign (AD 40)

D2.1. At length, as if about to go to war, he drew up a line of battle on the shore of the Ocean, deploying *ballistae* (catapults) and other artillery. No one knew or imagined what he could be going to do, when he suddenly ordered them to gather up shells and to fill their helmets and the laps of their tunics. He called them "spoils from the Ocean, dues to the Capitol and Palatine". As a monument of his victory he erected a high tower, from which fires were to shine out at night as a guide to ships – just like the Pharos. Then, announcing a donation of a hundred denarii to each soldier, as if he were showing unprecedented liberality, he said: "Go on your way both happy and rich".

[Suetonius, *Caligula* 46.1]

The Pharos was the famous lighthouse at Alexandria (Egypt).

D2.2. [59.25.1] When Caligula reached the Ocean, as if he were about to advance into Britain, he drew up his soldiers on the beach. [2] He then embarked on a trireme, putting out from the shore and then sailing back again. Then he took his seat on a lofty platform, and gave the soldiers the signal as for battle, ordering the trumpeters to urge them on. Then suddenly he ordered them to pick up sea-shells. [3] Having secured these spoils, for it was evident that he needed booty for his triumphal procession, he became greatly elated, as if he had subdued the Ocean itself. He gave many presents to his soldiers. He took back the shells to Rome, in order to exhibit his booty there as well.

[Cassius Dio, *Roman History* 59.25.1–3]

Other mentions of Caligula's attempted campaign can be found in Tacitus, *Agricola* 13 and Orosius, *History against the Pagans* 7.5.5. It is not clear why the campaign, possibly connected with Adminius' surrender, was aborted.

THE FIRST CENTURY, AD 41–98

E.   CLAUDIUS (AD 41–54)

E1.   Pomponius Mela's description of Britain (AD 43)

[3.49] What sort of place Britannia is and the sort of men it produces will soon be stated with more certainty and based on better information. For, lo and behold, the greatest *princeps* has opened an island for so long closed. The conqueror of peoples, previously not merely undefeated but actually unknown, carries the tangible proofs of what he set out to achieve in war to be proclaimed in his triumph.

[50] Otherwise, as we have thought before, with a corner at an obtuse angle overlooking the harbours of the Rhine, Britannia stretches out towards the north and west, then the sloping side slants back. Thus the island faces Gaul on one side, Germany on the other; then again on the uninterrupted edge of the straight shoreline, sloping down from its back, it forms an irregular triangle, three-sided and very similar in shape to Sicily. Britannia is flat, large and fertile, especially for those raising flocks rather than men.

[51] Britannia provides forests and glades, huge rivers which, with changing tides sometimes flow into the sea, sometimes back, and some which produce gemstones and pearls. There are tribes and kings of tribes, but all are uncivilised. The further away from the mainland they are, the more ignorant of finer resources; rich only in sheep and territory, their bodies painted with woad, whether to make them look better or for some other purpose.

[52] However they stir up causes of war and wars themselves, and frequently attack each other, especially in desire to be in command and out of eagerness to extend the lands they possess. They fight not only on horseback or on foot, but also from chariots and vehicles armed in the Gallic fashion: they call these *covinni* which use blades on the axles.

[53] Beyond Britannia is Iuverna [*Hibernia, Ireland*], almost equal in size, but oblong in shape with an equal length of shore on each side. Its climate is not suitable for crops to ripen, but the island is so luxuriant with grasses which are sweet as well as juicy, that flocks eat their fill in only a short part of the day, and would burst from grazing too long unless kept away from fodder. The inhabitants are rough and ignorant of virtues to an even greater degree than other tribes, and completely lacking in religious piety.

[Pomponius Mela, *Geography* 3.49–53]

Pomponius Mela wrote the first work on geography in Latin, which he published, as the passage implies, soon after Claudius' invasion of Britain. Mela's information derives from earlier writers including Caesar, *Gallic Wars* (see **A1–10, A16** above: chariots, woad, Kent is more civilised), Diodorus Siculus (**A15**: orientation of Britain, shape like Sicily), and Strabo (**B3**: Irish lack of piety). The unlikely tradition of axle-blades (as on Boudicca's statue in London) seems to originate with Mela.

E2. The invasion of Britain (AD 43)

E2.1. [17.1] He undertook only one expedition, and that a modest one. The Senate had decreed him triumphal ornaments, but he regarded this as beneath his dignity as emperor. He sought the honour of a real triumph, and chose Britain as the best field in which to seek this, for no one had attempted an invasion since the time of Julius Caesar and the island at this time was in turmoil because certain refugees had not been returned to the island. [2] Voyaging from Ostia he was twice nearly drowned by north-westerly storms, once off Liguria and again off the Stoechades islands. So he finished the journey from Massilia [*Marseilles*] to Gesoriacum [*Boulogne*] by land. Crossing from there he received the submission of part of the island within a very few days without either battle or bloodshed.

[Suetonius, *Claudius* 17.1–2]

E2.2. [7.13.2] Claudius waged war on Britain, where no Roman had set foot since the days of Gaius Caesar, and when the country had been vanquished by Gnaeus Sentius and Aulus Plautius, distinguished members of noble families, he held a magnificent triumph. [3] He also added to the Roman Empire certain islands in the Ocean beyond Britain, called the Orchades, and gave his son the name Britannicus.

[Eutropius, *Brief History* 7.13.2–3]

Eutropius wrote a brief account (in Latin) of Roman history from Romulus to AD 364, his own time.

See also Orosius, *History against the Pagans* 7.6.9–10 on Claudius' need for a military triumph, and Seneca *ad Polybium* 13.1–2 on the enthusiasm for military operations in Britain. Other references to the invasion are Suetonius, *Vitellius* 2.4 and Tacitus, *Agricola* 13.

The invasion army: see **E3–E6** below; also *L4* 7–18, 278–279.
Entourage of Claudius: Suetonius, *Claudius* 28; *Galba* 7.1; Tacitus, *Annals* 11.3.
The client kingdoms: Tacitus, *Agricola* 14.2; *L4* 137; Tacitus, *Annals* 12.31 (**E8** below); 12.40 (**E14** below); Seneca, *Apocolocyntosis* 12.3.

E3. Verica appeals to Claudius; Aulus Plautius leads the invasion force and lands unopposed

E3.1. [60.19.1] Aulus Plautius, a senator of great reputation, led an expedition to Britain. This was because a certain Berikos [*Verica*], who had been driven out of the island as a result of civil war, persuaded Claudius to send a force there. [2] Thus it came about that Plautius undertook the campaign, but he had difficulty in persuading his army to leave Gaul. The soldiers objected to the idea of campaigning outside the limits of the civilised world, and would not obey Plautius until Narcissus, who had been sent out by Claudius, mounted Plautius' tribunal and attempted to address them. [3] At first they were angry at this and would not allow Narcissus to say anything. But suddenly they shouted in unison "Io Saturnalia", for at the Saturnalia slaves don their master's dress and hold a festival, and returned to their obedience to Plautius. However, their mutiny had made their departure late in the season.

[Cassius Dio, *Roman History* 60.19.1–3]

Coin evidence for Verica includes *L4* 4, a gold stater.

Narcissus was one of Claudius' imperial freedmen.

E3.2.   [60.19.4] They were sent over in three divisions, so that their landing should not be hindered, as might have happened with a single force. On the way across, they were at first discouraged, because they were driven back on their course, but they recovered when they saw a flash of light shoot across the sky from east to west, the direction in which they were travelling. When they reached the island they found no one to oppose them. [5] On the strength of the reports they received the Britons had concluded that they were not coming and had not assembled to meet them. Even when they did assemble, they refused to come to close quarters with the Romans, but fled to the swamps and forests, hoping to wear out the enemy and force him to sail away again, just as they had done in the time of Julius Caesar.

[Cassius Dio, *Roman History* 60.19.4–5]

E4.   Plautius engages the British and crosses the River Medway

[60.20.1] So Plautius had a lot of trouble in finding them, but when at last he did, he first defeated Caratacus and then Togodumnus, the sons of Cunobelinus, who was now dead. The Britons were not free and independent, but were ruled by various kings. [2] After these had fled, he won over a section of the Bodounni, who were subject to the Catuvellauni. Then, leaving behind a garrison, he continued his advance. He came to a river which the barbarians thought the Romans would be unable to cross without a bridge; in consequence they had camped in careless fashion on the far bank. But Plautius sent across a detachment of Germans, who were accustomed to swimming in full equipment across the strongest streams. [3] They fell unexpectedly on the enemy, but instead of attacking the men they concentrated on their chariot-horses. In the ensuing confusion not even the enemy's mounted men escaped. Plautius thereupon sent across Flavius Vespasianus, who afterwards became emperor, and his brother Sabinus who was serving under him. [4] They managed to get across the river and surprised and killed many of the enemy. However the survivors did not take to flight. On the next day they joined battle again. The struggle was indecisive, until Gaius Hosidius Geta, after a narrow escape from capture, fell upon the Britons to such effect that he was later awarded the triumphal ornaments, even though he had not yet held the consulship.

[Cassius Dio, *Roman History* 60.20.1–4]

The Bodounni are most likely the Dobunni, a tribe based in south-west England with their capital at Cirencester (Corinium Dobunnorum).
See E6 and G1.5 below for more on Vespasian's service in Britain.

E5.   Plautius crosses the River Thames after killing Togodumnus, and sends for Claudius

E5.1.   [60.20.5] The Britons now fell back on the river Thames, at a point near where it enters the sea, and at high tide forms a pool. They crossed over easily because they knew where to find firm ground and an easy passage. [6] But the Romans in trying to follow them were not so successful. However, the Germans again swam across, and other troops got over by a bridge a little upstream, after which they attacked the barbarians from several sides at once, and killed many of their number. But in pursuing the remainder incautiously some of the troops got into difficulties in the marshes, and a number were lost.

[*Cassius Dio, Roman History* 60.20.5–6]

E5.2.   [60.21.1] Because of this, and because even though Togodumnus had perished, the Britons, far from yielding, had united all the more firmly to avenge him, Plautius was afraid to advance further. He proceeded to consolidate what he had gained, and sent for Claudius. [2] He had been instructed to do this if he met any particularly strong opposition, and indeed considerable equipment, including elephants, had already been assembled as reinforcements. On receiving this message Claudius committed affairs in Rome, including the command of the troops, to his fellow-consul Lucius Vitellius, whom he had kept in office, like himself, for the full half-year, and set out for Britain. [3] Sailing down the river to Ostia, he followed the coast to Massilia [*Marseilles*]. [4] Thence he progressed, partly by road and partly by river, until he came to the Ocean. Crossing over to Britain he joined the troops that were waiting for him at the Thames. Taking over the command of these troops he crossed the river and engaged the barbarians who had assembled to oppose him; he defeated them, and captured Camulodunum, the capital of Cunobelinus. After this he won over a number of tribes, some by diplomacy, some by force, and was saluted as Imperator several times, contrary to precedent, [5] for no one may receive this title more than once for any one war. He deprived those who submitted of their arms, and putting these people under the control of Plautius, he ordered him to subdue the remaining areas. He himself now hastened back to Rome, sending on the news of his victory by his sons-in-law Magnus and Silanus.

[*Cassius Dio, Roman History* 60.21.1–5]

E6.   Vespasian's role in the Claudian invasion

E6.1.   [4.1] In the reign of Claudius, Vespasian became legate of a legion in Germany by the favour of Narcissus. Crossing with the legion to Britain, he fought the enemy thirty times. He conquered two of the strongest tribes, captured more than twenty towns (*oppida*) and also the Isle of Wight, partly under the command of Claudius, partly under the consular legate Aulus Plautius. [2] For this he was awarded triumphal ornaments and shortly afterwards two priesthoods. In addition he was made consul for the last two months of the year (*in AD 51*).

[Suetonius, Vespasian 4.1–2]

Vespasian commanded the Second Legion: see G1.5 below.
One of the *oppida* was Maiden Castle (Dorset), where remains of the British dead have been found.

E6.2.   [3.4] Nero could find no one but Vespasian equal to the situation [*the Jewish revolt*], and capable of undertaking a campaign on such a scale. He had been a soldier from his youth, and had grown grey in the service. Earlier in his career he had pacified the west and rescued it from harassment by the Germans; with his troops he had added

Britain, until then almost unknown, to the empire, [5] and thus provided Claudius, the father of Nero, with a triumph which cost him no personal exertion.

[Josephus, *Jewish War* 3.4–5]

Josephus was a Jewish rebel leader in the revolt of AD 66–74 who had changed sides and gained the patronage of Vespasian and Titus. His history of the revolt (written in Aramaic, then translated by him into Greek) flatters Vespasian and Titus and magnifies Vespasian's earlier achievements.

Other accounts of Vespasian's role, all complimentary: Tacitus, *Agricola* 13.5; *Histories* 3.44 (**G1.5** below); Silius Italicus, *Punic War* 3.597–600; Valerius Flaccus, *Argonautica* 1.7; Cassius Dio 65.8.3; Eutropius 7.19. Cassius Dio 60.30.1 has a story of Vespasian being encircled by the Britons but rescued by his son Titus, which is implausible because Titus (born in 39) was a child at the time; the episode may belong to the Jewish War.

E7. Claudius's triumph and other victory celebrations

See also Pliny, *Natural History* 3.119 = *L19* N17; Cassius Dio 60.25.7–8. Coins commemorating the victory: *L4* 20 (AD 46/7). Victory crowns received by Claudius: Pliny, *Natural History* 33.54; *L4* 21 (AD 46).

E7.1. [17.2] Within six months he had returned to Rome, where he celebrated his triumph with the greatest pomp. [3] To witness the spectacle he permitted not only provincial governors to come to Rome, but even certain exiles. And among the symbols of victory he fixed a Naval Crown next to the Civic Crown on the gable of the Palace, a token that he had crossed and as it were conquered the Ocean. His wife Messalina followed his triumphal chariot in a carriage *(carpentum)*. Those who had won triumphal ornaments in the war also followed, but on foot, and in purple-bordered togas, except Marcus Crassus Frugi, who wore a tunic decorated with palms and rode on a horse decorated with medallions *(phalerae)*, because this was the second time that he had won the honour.

[Suetonius, *Claudius* 17.2–3]

"Conquest of Ocean": *ILS* 212 (AD 48) = *L19* M11c, compare Tacitus, *Annals* 11.23–5 = *L19* M12

E7.2. [60.22.1] The Senate on hearing of this achievement voted him the title Britannicus, and gave him permission to hold a triumph. They also voted an annual festival to commemorate the event, and decreed that two triumphal arches should be erected, one in Rome and one in Gaul, since it was from Gaul that he had crossed over into Britain. [2] They bestowed upon his son the same title, and indeed in a way Britannicus came to be the boy's usual name. Messalina was granted the right of using a front seat at the theatre which Livia had enjoyed, and also the right of using a carriage *(carpentum)* in the city.

[Cassius Dio, *Roman History* 60.22.1–2]

Triumphal arches: *L4* 22 (AD 51).

E7.3. [60.23.1] Thus were parts of Britain conquered. Later, in the consulship of Gaius Crispus (for the second time) and Titus Statilius [AD 44], Claudius came back to Rome after an absence of six months, of which he spent only sixteen days in Britain, and celebrated his triumph. In this he followed precedent, even ascending the steps of the Capitol on his knees, with his sons-in-law supporting him on either side. [2] He granted to the senators who had campaigned with him the triumphal ornaments, and this not only to those who were of consular rank... [4] After attending to these matters, he celebrated his triumph... [6] These things were done on account of events in Britain, and in order that other tribes should the more readily come to terms, it was decreed that all agreements made by Claudius or his legates should be as binding as if they had been made by the Senate and People.

[Cassius Dio, *Roman History* 60.23.1–6]

E7.4.   The emperor extended the city boundary (*pomerium*) in accordance with the ancient custom whereby anyone who had extended the power of Rome was permitted to extend the boundaries of the city. The right had not been exercised by Roman commanders even though they had subdued mighty nations, except for Lucius Sulla and the deified Augustus. (*AD 49*)

[Tacitus, *Annals* 12.23]

Extension of *pomerium*: *ILS* 213 = *L19* N24; *ILS* 244.12–16; Aulus Gellius, *Attic Nights* 13.14.7 = *L19* N23

E7.5.   He gave a show in the Campus Martius representing the siege and capture of a town (*oppidum*) in the manner of a real war, as well as of the surrender (*deditio*) of the kings of the Britons. He presided clad in a general's cloak.

[Suetonius, *Claudius* 21.6]

E7.6.   For his skilful and successful conduct of operations in Britain Plautius was not only praised by Claudius but was allowed a triumph.

[Cassius Dio, *Roman History* 60.30.2]

E7.7.   He also decreed an ovation to Aulus Plautius, going out to greet him when he entered the City, and "giving him the wall" as he went to the Capitol and returned again.

[Suetonius, *Claudius* 24.3]

Ovation of Plautius, AD 47: Tacitus, *Annals* 13.32 – not a triumph, as claimed by Cassius Dio (**E7.6** above) and Eutropius 7.13 = *L19* N15.

E8.   Ostorius Scapula becomes governor, disarms the tribes and puts down a revolt led by the Iceni (AD 47–48)

In Britain the propraetor, Publius Ostorius, was faced with a chaotic situation. The enemy had poured into our allies' territory all the more violently because they thought that a new commander, with an unfamiliar army and winter coming on, would not confront them. Ostorius knew that it is initial results which produce fear or confidence, and he swept his mobile auxiliary units into battle, cutting down those who resisted, scattering and pursuing the enemy; he wanted to prevent them from regrouping and to avoid a tense and treacherous peace which would allow no rest to either commander or soldiers. He disarmed those whose loyalty was suspect and prepared to consolidate the whole area this side of the Trent and the Severn.

It was the Iceni, a strong tribe who had not been broken on the field of battle because they had allied themselves with us voluntarily, who were the first to rebel against this. Under their leadership the tribes of that area selected for battle a place which was protected by a rough rampart and a narrow approach which made it inaccessible to cavalry. The Roman commander set about the task of breaking through these defences, although he had only allied forces with him without legionary support. He made his dispositions with his infantry and also apportioned duties to the dismounted cavalry. Then at a signal the soldiers forced their way through the rampart and threw into confusion an enemy hindered by their own defences. The British performed many valiant deeds, with rebellion on their consciences and their escape-routes blocked, and in this battle the governor's son, Marcus Ostorius, won the decoration for saving the life of a Roman citizen.

[Tacitus, *Annals* 12.31]

This battle may have been the one thought to have occurred at Stonea Camp, a hillfort in Cambridgeshire, where human remains with visible sword marks have been found.

Tacitus, *Agricola* 14.1–2 describes briefly events in the years AD 47–60.

E9.   A revolt by the Brigantes is suppressed and a colony is founded at Camulodunum to maintain peace in eastern Britain during hostilities against the Silures (*c.* AD 49)

Those who had been wavering between war and peace settled down after the disaster which had overtaken the Iceni, and the army moved against the Decangi. Their country was laid waste and booty gathered on every side. The enemy did not venture into battle or, if they did emerge from hiding to harass our line, they were punished for their treachery. The army had reached a point not far from the sea facing the island of Ireland when trouble broke out among the Brigantes and forced the commander to return; he had determined on a policy of not undertaking new conquests unless his previous ones were secure. The Brigantes in fact settled down after those who had begun to take up arms were killed and pardon extended to the rest; but no severity, no leniency made any difference to the Silures; there was nothing for it but to make war on them and hold them down with a legionary garrison. In order to achieve that more easily a colony (*colonia*) was founded on captive territory at Camulodunum. This was a strong settlement of veterans intended as a reserve against rebellion and to instil in our allies the habit of observing the laws.

[Tacitus, *Annals* 12.32]

The colony at Camulodunum (Colchester, Essex) is also mentioned in Tacitus, *Agricola* 14.1 and as a reason for the Trinovantes joining the Boudiccan rebellion in **F3.2** below.
The Decangi were probably based in North Wales/Cheshire.

E10. Caratacus leads the Silures and Ordovices against the Romans; Ostorius defeats Caratacus' forces (*c.* AD 50)

[12.33] Then the offensive was launched against the Silures. This naturally warlike tribe was further inspired by the power of Caratacus who, as a result of many battles in which he had matched or defeated the Romans, had reached a pre-eminent position among British chieftains. As he had fewer troops than us but was better placed to use local knowledge for his treacherous purposes, he proceeded to transfer the war into the territory of the Ordovices, where he was joined by those who feared a Roman peace. Here he made his last stand. He chose for battle a site that was difficult to approach but easy to abandon, and in every other respect suited his men rather than ours. On one side were high mountains and wherever there was a more gradual incline he constructed a barrier of stones like a rampart. This was behind a river which had no safe crossing-points, and in front of the fortifications armed men had taken up their positions.

[34] At this point the leaders of the tribes went round haranguing their men and stiffening their resolve; they allayed their fears, kindled their hopes and used all the other inducements known to military leaders; indeed Caratacus sped round to every part to declare that this was the day, this was the battle which would restore their liberty or make them slaves for ever; he invoked the names of their ancestors who had routed the dictator Caesar; it was due to their valour that they now enjoyed freedom from Roman authority and tribute, and their wives and children were unmolested. The men roared their approval when he made these and similar utterances and they bound themselves man by man by their tribal oaths not to yield to weapons or wounds.

[35] This enthusiasm dismayed the Roman commander; and at the same time he was awed by the obstacle of the river, the rampart which had been added behind it, the overhanging hills, the danger that threatened on every side and the thronging bands of enemy defenders. But his soldiers demanded battle; they shouted that with courage everything could be taken by storm; and officers of every rank, saying the same thing, intensified the ardour of the army. Then Ostorius, after reconnoitring to see where an approach was practicable and where not, led his determined army forward and crossed the river without difficulty. When they reached the rampart and were fighting with missiles, the wounds were mainly on our side and quite a number of men were killed; but our men formed a tortoise-shell formation and tore down the rough and loosely built wall, and in the hand-to-hand fighting the armies were evenly matched. The enemy withdrew onto the slopes of the hills. But there too we broke through their lines; the light-armed troops attacked with their spears, the heavy-armed troops advanced in close formation, and the British troops, unprotected as they were by breastplates or helmets, were put to flight before them. If they stood up to the auxiliaries, they fell before the swords and javelins of the legionaries, and if they turned elsewhere they were struck down by the broad swords and spears of the auxiliaries. It was a famous victory; Caratacus' wife and daughter were taken prisoners and his brothers gave themselves up.

[Tacitus, *Annals* 12.33–35]

E11.   Caratacus seeks sanctuary with Cartimandua but is handed over to the Romans; he appears in Rome and is pardoned by Claudius (AD 51)

[12.36]   Caratacus himself, vulnerable as those who have failed always are, sought the support of the queen of the Brigantes, Cartimandua, but was thrown into chains and handed over. This was the ninth year of the British war, and Caratacus' reputation, which had spread from the islands through the neighbouring provinces, was also well-known in Italy; men were eager to see this man who had mocked the power of Rome for so many years. At Rome too his name commanded respect, and even the Emperor, by making much of his own achievement, brought renown on his vanquished enemy. The people were summoned for a great spectacle. The praetorian cohorts stood to arms on the parade-ground which lay before the camp; Caratacus' client princelings processed, and the decorations and torques which he had won in his foreign wars were carried on; then appeared his brothers, wife and daughters, and finally Caratacus himself. The others were afraid and their prayers undignified; but Caratacus did not lower his eyes or beg for sympathy, and when he stood at the tribunal he spoke in the following way:

[37]   "If my noble birth and situation in life had been matched by only moderate success, I should have come to this city as a friend rather than a captive, and you would not have scorned to conclude a treaty with one sprung from famous ancestors and holding sway over many nations; my present lot degrades me, just as it brings glory to you. I had horses, men, arms, wealth; is it surprising that I was unwilling to lose them? You may want to rule over all men, but does it follow that all men welcome servitude? But if I had surrendered at once and so become your prisoner, little fame would have attended my fate and your renown would not have shone more brightly; sentence could be passed and everything forgotten; as it is you can preserve my life, and I shall be an example of your mercy for ever."

In reply the Emperor conferred pardon on Caratacus himself, his wife and brothers. On being freed from their chains they honoured Agrippina, who was sitting for all to see on another platform not far off, with the same praises and thanks which they offered to the Emperor. It certainly was a novelty, and not in accordance with the customs of our ancestors, that a woman should preside at a parade of the Roman standards; she was conducting herself like a partner in the empire which had been won by her ancestors.

[38] After that the Senate met and many fine speeches were made on the subject of Caratacus' capture; it was as glorious an occasion, it was said, as when Syphax was exhibited by Scipio Africanus, or Perseus by Aemilius Paulus, or all the other instances of foreign kings who were brought in chains before the Roman people; and triumphal ornaments were conferred by decree upon Ostorius.

[Tacitus, *Annals* 12.36–38]

The Britons may have honoured Agrippina on the mistaken assumption that women at Rome could hold royal power as they could in Britain.
Syphax, a Numidian king, was paraded in Rome in 201 BC; Perseus king of Macedon, in 167 BC.

E12.   The Silures continue to fight; Ostorius dies (AD 51)

[12.38] The success which had so far attended Ostorius presently began to desert him. Either the campaign flagged on our side, as though, with the removal of Caratacus, the war was thought to have been brought to a successful conclusion, or else the enemy grieved at the loss of so great a king and burned all the more fiercely to avenge him. Some legionary cohorts under a camp commandant had been left behind to build forts on Silurian territory; these were surrounded, and if help had not come quickly from neighbouring forts in response to the alert, the beleaguered forces would have been cut down; as it was the commander, eight centurions and the best of the men from the ranks were killed.

Shortly afterwards the enemy scattered a Roman foraging party together with the cavalry squadrons sent to help them. [39] At this Ostorius brought up his light-armed auxiliaries, but even so would not have halted the rout if the legions had not entered the battle. Their strength evened up the fighting which ultimately went in our favour; but with night coming on the enemy escaped with little loss.

After this there were frequent battles, often taking the form of guerrilla warfare among the passes or marshes, brought on variously by chance or valour; these engagements might be spontaneous or planned, for revenge or booty, sometimes in accordance with the orders of an officer and sometimes not. The stubbornness of the Silures was remarkable and they were incensed by a widely-reported saying of the Roman commander that the Silures must be totally eliminated, as had previously happened to the Sugambri, of whom those who were not destroyed were removed to Gaul. They therefore cut off two auxiliary cohorts which through the greed of their commanders were plundering without due precautions, and by freely distributing the spoils and captives they drew other nations into the rebellion. Worn out by the worry of his responsibilities, Ostorius died, and the enemy rejoiced. It looked as if a commander of some account had fallen as a casualty of the war, even if not on the field of battle.

[Tacitus, *Annals* 12.38–39]

E13.   Aulus Didius Gallus becomes governor (AD 52) and finally defeats the Silures

On receiving the news of the commander's death the Emperor appointed Aulus Didius to replace him, so that the province would not be without a governor. He made the journey quickly but he found affairs in an unsatisfactory state; the legion commanded by Manlius Valens had been worsted; the enemy exaggerated their account of the event in order to frighten the incoming commander, and he exaggerated the accounts brought to him whether to increase his own renown if he settled the matter, or to swell the sympathy that he might expect if the enemy continued to hold out. The Silures again had inflicted that loss and they ranged far and wide until they were driven off by Didius' arrival.

[Tacitus, *Annals* 12.40]

E14.   Civil war amongst the Brigantes; the Romans assist Cartimandua

After the capture of Caratacus, the one who excelled in military skill was Venutius from the nation of the Brigantes, as I have said above. For a long time he was loyal and enjoyed the protection of Roman arms; but this was while he was married to the queen, Cartimandua, and after a rift between them the war that immediately ensued also threatened us. Initially, however, they only fought among themselves, and Cartimandua with some cunning ruses captured Venutius' brother and relations. The enemy were infuriated at this, and were further provoked by the disgrace of being subjected to female rule; a strong and well-armed force of fighting men invaded her kingdom. We had foreseen this and auxiliaries which were sent to help took part in a fierce fight which began with victory hanging in the balance but ended more happily. There was a similar outcome to a battle fought by the legion under the command of Caesius Nasica; Didius, weighed down by old age and already rich in honours, was satisfied to act through subordinates and to hold off the enemy.

I have brought these events together, although they happened under two propraetors over a period of years [AD *47 – c. 52*], because in different sections they would be more difficult to remember.

[Tacitus, *Annals* 12.40]

'*As I have said above*': Venutius must have been mentioned in Tacitus' lost account of the years AD 43–46/7, which implies earlier Roman contact with the Brigantes.

E15.   Abolition of Druidism

He utterly abolished the awful and inhuman religion of the Druids among the Gauls, which under Augustus had merely been prohibited to Roman citizens.

[Suetonius, *Claudius* 25.5]

F.   NERO (AD 54–68)

F1.   Nero is uninterested in Britain

He was never at any time moved by any desire or hope of expanding the empire. He even contemplated withdrawing the army from Britain, and only desisted from his purpose because he did not wish to appear to belittle the glory of his father.

[Suetonius, *Nero* 18]

F2.   Events preceding Boudicca's revolt: Suetonius Paulinus becomes governor and attacks Anglesey (AD 60)

[14.29]   The following year, in the consulship of Caesennius Paetus and Petronius Turpilianus [AD *61*], a serious disaster was suffered in Britain. The governor there, Aulus Didius, as I have mentioned, had only held on to our existing conquests. His successor, Veranius, had ravaged Silurian territory with some limited expeditions when death prevented him from carrying the war any further. During his life, he had been famous for his austerity, but in his last words, expressed in his will, he betrayed his vanity, for as well as flattering Nero he added that he would have brought the province under the Emperor's control if he had lived for two years more. The next, however, to hold the governorship of Britain was Suetonius Paulinus, who was Corbulo's rival both in his skill in warfare and in common talk, which always makes comparisons. He was ambitious to vanquish the enemy and so match the glory won by Corbulo in the recovery of Armenia. He therefore prepared [AD 60] to attack the island of Mona [*Anglesey*], which was a native stronghold and a haven for fugitives, and built flat-bottomed boats to contend with the shallows and quicksands. These were to carry across the infantry; the cavalry followed by fording the channel or swimming beside their horses in the deeper waters.

[30] Standing on the shore before them were the enemy forces, a densely packed body of armed men; there were women running among them, dressed in funereal robes like Furies, with hair streaming and with torches in their hands; and round about them stood the Druids, raising their hands to heaven and pouring down terrible curses. The strangeness of this sight unnerved the soldiers, and they seemed to be paralysed; they presented their motionless bodies as a target; but then, urged on by their commander, and challenging each other not to be alarmed by a horde of frenzied women, they carried the standards forward, struck down those in their path and enveloped the enemy with fire from their own torches. After this a garrison was set over the conquered islanders and the groves destroyed which had been devoted to their barbarous and superstitious rites; for it was part of their religion to honour their altars with the blood of their prisoners and to consult the gods by means of human entrails.

[Tacitus, *Annals* 14.29–30]

Cn. Domitius Corbulo had been given a special command in late AD 54 to drive the Parthians out of Armenia and to restore Roman dominance; in AD 58–59 he had successfully invaded Armenia. For Paulinus' final two years as governor, see also Tacitus, *Agricola* 14.3.

Druids: see **A17, C1.2** and **E15** above.

F3.   Boudicca's rebellion (AD 60–61)

F3.1.   There were some chance misfortunes too, in addition to the disasters and abuses caused by the emperor: a single autumn's plague was responsible for 30,000 deaths being entered in the accounts of Libitina; there was the British disaster, in which large numbers of Roman citizens and their allies were slaughtered and two leading towns sacked.

[Suetonius, *Nero* 39.1]

F3.2.   While Suetonius was occupied with this [*conquering Anglesey; F2*], news arrived of a sudden rebellion in the province. Prasutagus, king of the Iceni, and a man distinguished for the wealth which he had enjoyed for many years, had made the Emperor his co-heir together with his two daughters, thinking that by such submission his kingdom and family would be kept from any harm. What happened was the reverse; his kingdom was plundered by centurions and his household by slaves, as if they were prizes of war. To begin with his wife, Boudicca, was whipped, and their daughters raped; all the leading Iceni were deprived of their ancestral property as if the Romans had been given the whole kingdom, and the king's relatives were treated like slaves. Smarting under this outrage and fearing that worse was to come when they became part of the province, the natives took up arms. The Trinobantes, together with others who had not yet been crushed by servitude, made a pact with secret oaths to win back their liberty and also rose in rebellion. They particularly detested the veterans, because the new colonists at Camulodunum had expelled them from their homes and driven them from their land, calling them prisoners and slaves. The soldiers encouraged the lawlessness of the veterans, for their way of behaving was the same, and they looked forward to the same freedom themselves. In addition to this the temple designated for the Divine Claudius was regarded as the stronghold of eternal Roman domination, while those chosen to serve as priests found their whole wealth drained away in the name of religion. To destroy the colony seemed no difficult task, as it had no defences; our commanders had paid too little attention to this, thinking more of what was pleasant to look at rather than what the town actually needed.

[Tacitus, *Annals* 14.31]

Colony at Camulodunum: see **E9** and Tacitus, *Agricola* 14.1.

F3.3.   This is the particular duty of an imperial procurator, that by his order an imperial slave can enter on an inheritance, and, if the Emperor is named as an heir, the procurator can effect this by involving himself in a rich inheritance.

[*Digest* 1.19.2 (Ulpian)]

Praustagus had become an ally of Rome and client of the emperor, so was expected to name his patron the emperor as an heir in his will; he probably hoped Nero would take some of his wealth but confirm his daughters as his successors.

Ulpian was a Roman jurist of the early 3rd century, whose works on Roman administrative law are often cited in the *Digest*.

F3.4.   [14.32] While this was going on, the statue of Victory at Camulodunum fell down, for no obvious reason, and its back was turned as though it were retreating from the enemy. Hysterical women began chanting of impending doom; barbarian cries, they said, had been heard in the senate-house; the theatre had echoed with the sound of wailing; the ghostly image of a colony in ruins had been seen in the Thames estuary. Now the sea took on a blood-red hue, and when the tide went out what appeared to be human corpses were left on the shore. The Britons interpreted these portents with hope, and the veterans with fear. Since Suetonius, however, was far away the veterans sought help from the procurator, Decianus Catus. He sent just two hundred men inadequately armed; in addition there was a small body of soldiers in the colony. The inhabitants relied on the temple for protection; hampered by those who secretly knew of the rebellion and were confusing their plans, they neither dug a ditch nor built a rampart. Further, the old people and women were not removed, so that only able-bodied men would remain; and when the town was surrounded by a horde of natives it was as if they had been caught unawares in a time of peace. After everything else had been plundered and burnt in the first onslaught the soldiers gathered in the temple, which was taken by storm after a siege of two days. The victorious Britons then went off to face Petilius Cerialis, legate of the Ninth Legion, who was hurrying to bring help; they routed the legion and killed what infantry there was with it, although Cerialis escaped with his cavalry to his fortress, seeking safety behind its fortifications. The procurator, Catus, frightened by this disaster and the hatred borne him by the provincials, whom he had driven to war through his greed, fled to Gaul.

[33] Suetonius, however, with extraordinary resolve, marched through hostile country to Londinium. This town had not been distinguished with the rank of colony, but was a very busy centre for businessmen and merchandise. He was uncertain whether he should choose this place as a base for the war; but, after considering the smallness of his army and the clear enough lesson to be learned from the check to Petilius' rash action, he decided to sacrifice a single town and preserve the province as a whole. The tears and wailing of those who begged for his help did not deter him from giving the signal to depart, although those who wished to were allowed to accompany the army; any who remained, either because they were women or too old to make the journey or too attached to the place, were massacred by the enemy. The township of Verulamium suffered the same fate, because the natives bypassed the forts, which were guarded by soldiers; glad of the chance of booty, and tired of their exertions, they made for the places which were most profitable to plunder and had no garrison to defend them. It is generally agreed that as many as seventy thousand Roman citizens and allies died at the places I have mentioned. The natives did not take or sell prisoners or carry out any of the exchanges which often take place in war; they hastened to cut down, hang, burn or crucify, as though they were seizing the opportunity for vengeance for the punishment which was ultimately bound to catch up with them.

[34] By this time Suetonius had the Fourteenth Legion with him which, together with detachments of the Twentieth and the nearest available auxiliary units, came to nearly ten thousand armed men. It was at this stage that he decided to delay no longer and to meet the enemy in pitched battle. His choice of position fell upon a narrow defile, blocked off at the rear by a wood. He made sure that there were no enemy anywhere save to his front, where the ground was open and there was no risk of ambush, and accordingly drew up the legionaries in close ranks with the light-armed auxiliary infantry on either side and his cavalry massed on the wings. On their side the British forces were moving excitedly all over the place in their groups of infantry and cavalry, and in larger numbers than had ever been seen before. They were in such confident spirits that they had also brought their wives with them to witness the victory, placing them in carts around the edges of the plain.

[35] Boudicca rode up to each tribe in a chariot with her daughters in front of her. "We British," she cried, "are used to women commanders in war. But it is not as the descendant of mighty ancestors that I fight now, avenging lost kingdom and wealth; rather as one of the people, avenging lost liberty, scourging, the violation of my daughters. The lusts of the Romans are gross; they cannot keep their filthy hands from our bodies, not even from the old or chaste. But the gods are at hand with a just revenge; the legion is destroyed which dared to face us in battle; the rest skulk in their camps, or watch for a chance to flee. They will not stand up before the noise and roar

of so many thousands, let alone the attack and the hand-to-hand fighting. Think of the number of our troops, think of why you fight – and you must either win on this battlefield or die. That is my resolve, and I am a woman; men may live and be slaves."

[36] By the same token Suetonius did not remain silent with so much in the balance; although he trusted in the bravery of his men, he still spoke to them with encouragement and appeals. "Pay no attention to the din and empty threats made by the natives," he said; "there are more women to be seen over there than fighting men. Poor soldiers, and unarmed, they have been routed by you many times; they will yield at once when they recognise the weapons and the courage of their conquerors. Even where many legions are present, it is only a few men who secure the victories; your glory will be all the greater if a small force gains the distinction of a whole army. Just keep in close formation, throw your javelins, and then follow through – knock them to the ground with your shield bosses and kill them with your swords. Don't think about plunder; when you have won, everything will be yours." Such enthusiasm greeted the general's words, and so ready were the veteran soldiers, with long experience of fighting behind them, to hurl their javelins, that Suetonius was confident of the outcome and gave the signal for battle.

[37] At first the legionaries did not move, keeping to the protection of the narrow defile, and they threw their javelins with unerring accuracy at the enemy who were advancing to attack. Then they burst forward in a wedge formation. At the same moment the auxiliary infantry attacked; and the cavalry, with their lances extended, broke through any strong opposition. The rest of the Britons fled, but their escape was made more difficult by the carts which they had placed around the battlefield, and which now blocked their paths. The soldiers did not refrain from killing women too, and even baggage animals were transfixed with spears and swelled the mound of bodies. It was a famous victory won on that day, equal to triumphs of old; some sources say that just under eighty thousand Britons died; Roman casualties were about four hundred dead, with a slightly larger number of wounded. Boudicca poisoned herself. Poenius Postumus, Camp Commandant of the Second Legion, when he learned of the success of the men of the Fourteenth and Twentieth Legions, fell on his sword, because he had cheated his legion of their share of glory and, contrary to military discipline, had disobeyed his commander's orders.

[Tacitus, *Annals* 14.32–37]

F3.5.   [62.1.1] While this child's play was going on at Rome, a fearful catastrophe took place in Britain; two cities were sacked, 80,000 of the Romans and their allies perished, and the island fell into enemy hands. It was especially shameful for the Romans that it was a woman who brought all this upon them. There had actually been divine warnings of the catastrophe; [1.2] there had been the sound at night of barbarians shouting and laughing in the senate-house, and uproar and lamentation in the theatre. But it was no mortal who had shouted or lamented. Houses were seen under the water in the river Thames. The high tide of the ocean between the island and Gaul on one occasion was blood-red.

[2.1] Claudius had given sums of money to the leading Britons, and according to Decianus Catus, the procurator of the island, this money had to be returned together with the rest. The confiscation of this money was the pretext for the war. In addition, Seneca, with a view to a good rate of interest, had lent the reluctant islanders 40,000,000 sesterces and had then called it all in at once, and not very gently. So rebellion broke out. [2.2] But above all the rousing of the Britons, the persuading of them to fight against the Romans, the winning of the leadership and the command throughout the war – this was the work of Buduica, a woman of the British royal family who had uncommon intelligence for a woman. [2.3] When she had collected an army about 120,000 strong, Buduica mounted a rostrum made in the Roman fashion of heaped-up earth. [2.4] She was very tall and grim; her gaze was penetrating and her voice was harsh; she grew her long auburn hair to the hips and wore a large golden torque and a voluminous patterned cloak with a thick plaid fastened over it. This was how she always dressed. Now, taking a spear too to add to her effect upon the entire audience, she made this speech:

[3.1] "Experience has taught you the difference between freedom and slavery. Some of you may have been led by your ignorance of which was better, to be taken in by the Romans' tempting promises. But now you have tried both – and you have learned how wrong you were to prefer a foreign tyranny to the way of life followed by your ancestors; you have discovered the difference between freedom in humble circumstances and slavery amidst riches. [3.2] Have we not suffered every variety of shameful and humiliating treatment from the moment that these people turned their attention to Britain? Have we not been deprived wholesale of our most important possessions, while paying taxes on the rest? [3.3] Do we not pasture and till all our other property for them and then pay an annual tax on our very lives? How much better it would have been to be traded as slaves once and for all rather than ransom ourselves each year and meaninglessly call ourselves free! How much better to have died by the sword than live and be taxed for it! But why do I speak of death? [3.4] Not even that is free with them; you know what we pay even for our dead."

[Cassius Dio, *Roman History* 62.1.1 – 62.3.4]

Child's play: Dio has just recounted the inauguration in AD 60 of the Neronia, a five-yearly festival of competitions in music, athletics and horse-racing.

Taxes: Dio makes Boudicca refer to the two main forms of direct taxation of provincials by Rome, both payable annually: levies in kind on farmland (*tributum soli*) and a poll-tax in cash (*tributum capitis*). Poll-tax records from Egypt show that if a taxpayer died in the first half of the year, his heirs were liable for half the poll-tax, and if he died in the second half, for the full annual charge.

Dio goes on to report (invent) more of Boudicca's speech (62.4–6), including her pulling a hare from her dress and attacking Nero for being a woman!

F3.6.   [62.7.1] So Buduica harangued the people. She then led her army against the Romans, who happened to be without a leader because the general Paulinus was campaigning in Mona [Anglesey], an island close to Britain. This gave her the chance to sack and plunder two Roman cities and perpetrate the indescribable slaughter to which I have already referred. [7.2] Every kind of atrocity was inflicted upon their captives, and the most fearful bestiality was when they hung up naked the noblest and best-looking women. They cut off their breasts and stitched them to their mouths, so that the women seemed to be eating them, and after this they impaled them on sharp stakes run right up the body. [7.3] While they were doing all this in the grove of Andate and other sacred places they performed sacrifices, feasted, and abandoned all restraint. Andate was their name for victory, and she enjoyed their especial reverence.

[8.1] Paulinus as it turned out had now conquered Mona, and when he heard of the disaster in Britain he lost no time in sailing back there from Mona. Fear of their numbers and their desperation made him reluctant to risk everything in an immediate battle with the barbarians; but although he was for delaying the battle to a more favourable moment he was short of corn and the barbarians kept up their attacks, and so he was forced unwillingly to engage them.

[8.2] Buduica had an army of about 230,000 men and made her way round in a chariot, assigning others to their various positions; Paulinus could not stretch his army out to face the whole enemy line – they were so outnumbered that they would not have covered the ground even with a line one deep – and he did not dare to fight in a single body for fear of being surrounded and cut down; so he divided his army into three with a view to fighting on several fronts at once, and drew up each division in close formation so that it would be hard to break up.

[9.1] As he gave his men their orders and positions he added words of exhortation. "Come, my fellow soldiers," he said; "come, Romans, show these murderers your superiority even in misfortune. You would be disgraced if your recent gains, courageously won, were now ignominiously lost. We and our fathers have often won against greater odds; [9.2] so do not be frightened by the numbers and enthusiasm of the rebels – the impetuosity that lends them courage is not supported by arms and training – or by their firing of some cities; they did not take them by force or in battle, but one after it had been betrayed and the other after it had been abandoned to them. Punish them for this now as they deserve, and let them discover by experience what sort of men they are compared with us, whom they have wronged."

[Cassius Dio, *Roman History* 62.7.1–9.2]

Dio goes on to report other speeches of Paulinus to different sections of his army (62.10–11).

F3.7.   [62.12.1] After making this and similar speeches he raised the signal for battle; and the two sides moved in to attack. The barbarians uttered loud yells and threatening chants, while the Roman advance was silent and disciplined. [2] But when they were within javelin-range, the Romans at a signal leapt forward simultaneously against the enemy, who were still walking, and charged them with great force; in the fighting they easily broke through the line facing them, even though they were surrounded by the great numbers of the enemy and were fighting on all sides at once.

[3] The struggle took many forms. Light-armed troops engaged with their counterparts. Cavalry charged cavalry, while the Roman archers were dealing with the barbarian chariots. The barbarians would sweep up in their chariots against the Romans, rout them, and would then themselves, fighting as they were without breastplates, be put to

flight by arrows. Cavalry threw the infantry into confusion, infantry struck down the cavalry. [4] Here the Romans made some progress by closing up their ranks to face the chariots, but in other places they were scattered by them. The archers were sometimes routed when the Britons came to grips with them, but in other places the barbarians kept out of their way. All this went on not just in one place but with all three divisions.

[5] There was a mighty battle and equal spirit and daring were shown by both sides. But at last, late in the day, the Romans prevailed; many of the enemy were killed in the fighting both beside their chariots and near the wood, and many more were taken alive. [6] Large numbers also escaped and prepared to fight again, but while they were making their preparations Buduica became ill and died. The Britons missed her sorely and gave her a lavish funeral; but in the belief that now they really were defeated they scattered to their homes.

[Cassius Dio, *Roman History* 62.12.1–6]

See also Tacitus, *Agricola* 5; 14.3–16.2, which records Agricola's service as military tribune under Suetonius Paulinus.

F4.   Nero's response to the rebellion

F4.1.   Then after drawing the whole army together, Suetonius kept it under canvas to finish the war. The Emperor increased his forces by sending over from Germany two thousand legionaries, eight cohorts of auxiliary infantry and a thousand cavalry. The arrival of the legionaries brought the Ninth Legion up to full strength, while the auxiliary troops, both cavalry and infantry, were placed in new winter quarters. The territory of any tribe which had either wavered in its allegiance, or been openly hostile, was laid waste by fire and sword; but it was famine which caused the natives the greatest hardship, since they had neglected to sow their crops, calling up men of every age to fight, and intending to take over our food supplies for themselves. The fiercest tribes were less inclined to lay down their arms because Julius Classicianus, who had been sent to replace Catus, disagreed with Suetonius and was obstructing the common good because of this personal feud. He put it about that it was worth waiting for a new governor, one who, without the animosity of an enemy or the arrogance of a conqueror, would look sympathetically on those who surrendered. He also sent despatches to Rome saying that they could expect no end to the hostilities unless Suetonius were replaced. He attributed the commander's failures to perverseness and his successes to luck.

[Tacitus, *Annals* 14.38]

Tombstone of Julius Classicianus, procurator AD 61–65: *L4* 24.

F4.2.   Therefore Polyclitus, one of the Emperor's freedmen, was sent to examine the position in Britain. Nero had high hopes that Polyclitus' influence would not only create harmony between governor and procurator, but also cure the natives' rebelliousness. Polyclitus managed to burden Italy and Gaul with an enormous entourage, and when he had crossed the Channel his progress inspired fear even in the Roman army. Yet to the enemy he was a laughing stock. For them the flame of liberty still burned, and as yet they knew nothing of the power of freedmen; they were amazed that a commander and an army which had brought so great a war to a successful conclusion should obey a slave. Everything was put in its most favourable light in Polyclitus' report to the Emperor, and Suetonius was kept in charge. Subsequently, however, after the loss of a few ships and their crews, which had run aground, he was ordered to surrender his command as though the war were still dragging on. He was replaced by Petronius Turpilianus, who had just completed his consulship. Turpilianus neither aggravated the enemy, nor was he himself provoked, and he dignified this lazy inactivity with the honourable name of peace.

[Tacitus, *Annals* 14.39]

Petronius Turpilianus (consul in 61, compare **F2**): see also Tacitus, *Agricola* 16.3.
Army units in the Claudian-Neronian and early Flavian period: *L4* 9–12, 17, 19, 129, 181.

F5.   Titus' military service in Britain

Titus served as a military tribune both in Germany and Britain. He became well known as much for his unassuming conduct as for his hard work, as one can judge from the numerous statues and busts of him and inscriptions in both provinces.

[Suetonius, *Titus* 4.1]

The future emperor Titus, son of Vespasian, probably served in Britain around AD 61–63, perhaps arriving with the reinforcements from Germany (see **F4.1** above)

G.   VESPASIAN (AD 69–79)

G1.   The Year of the Four Emperors and Vespasian's accession (AD 69)

G1.1.   The British army remained quiet. During all the civil strife which followed, no other legions conducted themselves more correctly, whether this was because, at such a distance, they were divided from the rest of the world by the Ocean, or because, hardened by frequent fighting, they hated the enemy rather than each other.

[Tacitus, *Histories* 1.9]

G1.2.   [1.59] The legions in Britain declared without hesitation in favour of Vitellius. [60] Trebellius Maximus was then governor, a man hated and despised by the army for his avarice and meanness. There had been a long-standing dispute between him and Roscius Caelius, legate of the Twentieth Legion, now fanned into flames by the events of the civil wars. Trebellius charged Caelius with sedition and with the disruption of discipline. Caelius accused Trebellius of reducing the legionaries to poverty by his despoliations. As a result of this dissension between their officers, the morale of the army was destroyed. Discord reached the highest pitch. Trebellius was assailed by the insults of the auxiliary soldiers. When the cohorts and *alae* deserted him and gave their support to Caelius, Trebellius fled to Vitellius. But the province remained quiet in spite of the departure of the consular governor. The legates of the legions controlled affairs. In theory they had equal authority, but in practice the audacity of Caelius gave him the greater power.

[Tacitus, *Histories* 1.59–60]

On Trebellius Maximus see also Tacitus, *Agricola* 16.3–5.

G1.3.   Trebellius Maximus did not meet with the same favour from Vitellius. He had fled from Britain on account of the anger of the soldiers. Vettius Bolanus was sent in his place from among those in attendance on Vitellius.

[Tacitus, *Histories* 2.65]

G1.4.   It was judged expedient (by Vitellius) to send them (the Fourteenth Legion) back to Britain, whence they had been summoned by Nero.

[Tacitus, *Histories* 2.66]

XIV Gemina had been withdrawn by Nero for his eastern campaign *c.* AD 67. The legion was soon moved to the continent: Tacitus, *Histories* 4.68.

G1.5.   The troops in Britain generally favoured Vespasian, for he had been put in command of the Second Legion there by Claudius and had distinguished himself in battle, but it was not without some misgivings that the other legions, in which most of the centurions and soldiers had received promotion from Vitellius, gave up their allegiance to an emperor of proven qualities.

[Tacitus, *Histories* 3.44]

For Vespasian's role in the Claudian invasion see E6 above.

G2.   Civil war among the Brigantes

As a result of this dissension and the frequent rumours of the civil wars, the Britons revived their ambitions. The leader in this was Venutius, a man of barbarous spirit who hated the Roman power. In addition he had motives of personal hostility against queen Cartimandua. Cartimandua's rule over the Brigantes was based on her high birth. Her power had grown when she captured king Caratacus by treachery and handed him over to embellish the triumph of the emperor Claudius. The result was riches, and the self-indulgence which flowers in prosperity. Venutius had been her husband. Spurning him, she made his armour-bearer Vellocatus her husband, and her partner in government. The power of her house was immediately shaken to its foundations by this outrage. The people of the tribe declared for Venutius: only the passion and the savage temper of the queen supported the adulterer. Venutius therefore summoned his supporters. The Brigantes rallied to him, reducing Cartimandua to the last extremity. She besought Roman protection. Our *alae* and cohorts fought indecisive battles, but at length rescued the queen from danger. The kingdom went to Venutius; we were left with a war to fight.

[Tacitus, *Histories* 3.45]

G3. Vettius Bolanus, governor AD 69–71

G3.1. Others may have Decius or the return of Camillus pointed out to them; do you learn the example of your own mighty father, who, carrying out his commission, penetrated to Thule, barrier of the western waters, where always Hyperion grows weary.

[Statius, *Silvae* 5.2.53–56]

G3.2. What glory will exalt the plains of Caledonia, when an ancient native of that wild land tells you: "This was where your father used to administer justice. This is the mound from which he addressed his cavalry. Far and wide – do you see them? – he set look-out posts and forts, and he had the ditch put round these walls. Here are the presents and weapons he dedicated to the gods of war – you can make out the inscriptions still. Here is the breast-plate he put on at battle's summons; here is one he wrenched from a British king."

[Statius, *Silvae* 5.2.142–149]

Papinius Statius was a versatile poet of the age of Domitian. This poem of *c.* AD 96 honours Crispinus, the son of Vettius Bolanus. Vettius Bolanus' appointment is mentioned in **G1.3** above.

Agricola served in 70–73 as legate of the Twentieth Legion under Vettius Bolanus and his successor Petilius Cerealis in their conquest of the Brigantes: see Tacitus, *Agricola* 7.5–8, 16.6–17.3.

G4. Territorial conquest stalls

In nearly thirty years, exploration of Britain has not been carried by Roman arms beyond the vicinity of the Caledonian Forest.

[Pliny the Elder, *Natural History* 4.102]

Presumably written in the early 70s AD, within thirty years of the Claudian invasion.

H. TITUS (AD 79–81) and DOMITIAN (AD 81–96)

H1. Agricola

H1.1. [66.20.1] Also at that time there was another war in Britain, and Gnaeus Julius Agricola overran all the lands of the enemies there. He was the first Roman of whom we know to have learned the fact that Britain is surrounded by water. Some soldiers, who had mutinied and killed their centurions and tribune, [2] fled to ships, set sail and sailed round the western side of it, just as the waves and wind carried them and, coming from the other side, put in at the camps of the first side unawares. Following this, Agricola sent others to try to sail round, and learned from them too that it is an island. [3] These were the events in Britain, and Titus was acclaimed imperator for the fifteenth time because of them. However Agricola lived the rest of his life in disgrace and even poverty, because his achievements were too great for a governor. Finally he was killed by Domitian on these grounds, although he had received triumphal honours from Titus.

[Cassius Dio, *Roman History* 66.20.1–3]

In fact Agricola received triumphal honours from Domitian. Agricola was appointed Governor of Britain under Vespasian in AD 77/78, and continued under Titus and Domitian until AD 83/84. He had served twice before in Britain, as a military tribune under Suetonius Paulinus (see **F3** above) and in command of the Twentieth Legion under Vettius Bolanus and Petilius Cerealis (see **G3.2** above). His three postings are recounted in Tacitus' *Agricola*, a eulogising biography written after Agricola's death (Tacitus was Agricola's son-in-law), which downplays the achievements of previous governors; see also **H1.2** below. Agricola as Governor is mentioned in two inscriptions of AD 79–81 (*L4* 25, 28) and one writing-tablet (*L4* 286).

H1.2.   (*Review of the Flavian period*) Illyricum convulsed; the Gauls on the point of rebelling; Britain conquered, then allowed to slip from our grasp; the Sarmatians and the Suebi rising against us; defeats inflicted by, and on, the Dacians.

[Tacitus, *Histories* 1.2]

The comment on Britain almost certainly alludes to Agricola's recall by Domitian in AD 83/84, shortly after his defeat of the Caledonians at Mons Graupius.

H2.   Demetrius of Tarsus

H2.1.   Nonetheless, shortly before the Pythian Games celebrated when Callistratus held office in our own day [AD 83], two men travelling from opposite ends of the inhabited world met at Delphi. These were the scholar Demetrius, who was travelling home from Britain to Tarsus, and the Spartan Cleombrotus.

[Plutarch, *On the Disuse of Oracles* 2]

H2.2.   Demetrius said that of the islands around Britain many were widely scattered and sparsely inhabited; several were called after deities or heroes. He himself had been commissioned by the emperor to sail to the nearest of these lonely islands to make enquiries and observations; it only had a few inhabitants, and they were all holy men who were considered sacrosanct by the Britons.

[Plutarch, *On the Disuse of Oracles* 18]

Demetrius of Tarsus, a grammarian, was a member of Agricola's entourage: *L4* 126.

H3.   Javolenus Priscus

Seius Saturninus, a chief pilot from the British Fleet, in his will left Valerius Maximus, a captain, as his fiduciary heir, and requested him to restore the inheritance to his son Seius Oceanus when he reached sixteen years. Seius Oceanus died before he reached that age. Now Mallius Seneca, who says he is the maternal uncle of Seius Oceanus, requests these goods by right of next of kin. (*Javolenus opines that the inheritance belongs to Oceanus' heirs, not to Valerius Maximus.*)

[*Digest* 36.1.48 (Javolenus)]

This ruling of Javolenus Priscus, a distinguished Roman jurist, may date from his service as *legatus iuridicus* ('law-giving [deputy]-governor') of Britain around AD 84/5; see *L4* 127. This is the first documentary attestation of a British Fleet as a separate unit, which is also implied in Tacitus *Agricola* (e.g. 38: under a Prefect).

H4.   Sallustius Lucullus

(*Domitian put to death many senators, including*) Sallustius Lucullus, legate of Britain, because he permitted lances of a new type to be called Lucullan.

[Suetonius, *Domitian* 10.3]

Sallustius Lucullus succeeded Agricola as governor of Britain; this is the only reference to his demise.

Domitian withdrew the II Adiutrix for his Dacian campaigns during Lucullus' governorship, hence the need to relinquish Agricola's Caledonian conquests. The fortress at Inchtuthill was abandoned and the XX Valeria Victrix moved to the fortress at Chester vacated by II Adiutrix. However a few auxiliary outposts were maintained, such as Dalswinton, where it is known that extensive rebuilding works took place under Lucullus.

THE SECOND CENTURY, AD 98–193

J.   TRAJAN (AD 98–117) and HADRIAN (AD 117–138)

Trajan: there is no literary evidence of activity in Britain under Trajan except for two very brief references in Juvenal, *Satires* 4.126 and 14.196. The main development was the creation of the so-called Stanegate frontier, which incorporated the fort of Vindolanda from which the tablets come: see *L4* 273–277.

L4 33 of AD 122 shows that the *cohors I Cugernorum* had been given the honorific title 'Traiana', presumably for some military exploit in Britain under Trajan.

Some military bases were rebuilt in stone: e.g. Caerleon, *L4* 29, AD 100; York, *L4* 30, AD 108; Gelligaer, *L4* 31, AD 103–111.

J1.1.   [5.1] When he became emperor, Hadrian at once reverted to an earlier policy and concentrated on maintaining peace throughout the world; [2] for while those nations which had been subdued by Trajan were rebelling, the Moors also were making attacks, the Sarmatians were waging war, the Britons could not be kept under Roman control, Egypt was hard pressed by revolts, and Libya and Palestine were showing an eagerness for rebellion.

[*Historia Augusta, Hadrian* 5.1–2]

J.1.2.   Not to go too far back into ancient times, I will take examples from your own family. Was not a man of consular rank taken prisoner in Dacia under the command and auspices of your great-grandfather Trajan? Was not a consular also killed by the Parthians in Mesopotamia? And again, when your grandfather Hadrian was emperor, how many soldiers were killed by the Jews, how many by the Britons? *(written in AD 162)*

[Fronto, *Letter to Marcus on the Parthian War* (Loeb II p. 20) 2]

Marcus Aurelius' relation to Trajan and Hadrian was by a series of adoptions.
Marcus Cornelius Fronto, a senator (consul in AD 142) and great orator, had been tutor to the young Marcus Aurelius and remained a friend.
Hadrian: Military operations early in the reign: *L4* 32.

J2.   Hadrian's Wall

So, having reformed the army in an excellent manner, he set out for Britain. There he put right many abuses and was the first to build a wall, eighty miles long, to separate the barbarians and the Romans. (*AD 121 or 122*)

[*Historia Augusta, Hadrian* 11.2]

Replacement of Pompeius Falco as governor by Platorius Nepos in AD 122: *L4* 33.
The idea of linear frontiers within which all are Romans and outside which all are barbarians is more typical of the 4th century of the *Historia Augusta* than of Hadrian's era.
Inscriptions about building the wall: *L4* 34–43.

J3.   No value in conquering Scotland

The Romans have penetrated beyond the northern ocean to Britain, an island larger than a considerable continent. They rule the most important part of it – more than half – and have no need of the rest; in fact the part they have brings them in little money.

[Appian, *Roman History* preface.5]

Appian, an imperial procurator of the mid-2nd century, wrote (in Greek) histories of Rome's wars; his lost final book (according to his preface.15) summarised Rome's armed forces, revenues and expenditures.

J4.   Julius Severus, governor *c.* AD 132

Then indeed Hadrian sent his best generals against the Jews. First of these was Julius Severus, who was sent from Britain, where he had been governor, to deal with them.

[Cassius Dio, *Roman History* 69.13.2]

Military campaigning: *ILS* 2726 = *L* 47; *ILS* 2735 = *L* 46; Cassius Dio 69.13.2.
Other references to campaigns in Britain in Hadrian's reign: *L4* 46–47.

K.   ANTONINUS PIUS (AD 138–161)

K1.1.   Antoninus waged many wars, using his legates. Lollius Urbicus, a legate, conquered the Britons for him, and when he had driven off the barbarians, built another wall, of turf.

[*Historia Augusta, Antoninus Pius* 5.4]

K1.2.   [3] Antoninus never willingly made war; but when the Moors took up arms against Rome he drove them from the whole of their territory … [4] Also in Britain he appropriated most of the territory of the Brigantes, because they too had begun a war by invading Genunia, which is subject to the Romans.

[Pausanias, *Description of Greece* 8.43.3–4]

Pausanias wrote his guidebook to the monuments of Greece in the mid-2nd century AD. Here he digresses from an account of Pallantion in Arcadia, favoured by Antoninus.

K1.3.   Thus Fronto, almost the most shining example of Roman eloquence, when he was giving Antoninus the credit for finishing the war in Britain, claimed that although the emperor stayed in his palace in Rome and delegated responsibility for the war, he deserved the glory for the whole start and progress of the expedition as though he had taken charge of the steering of a warship.

[*Panegyric of Constantius* 14.2]

Fronto: see **J1.2** above. For the panegyric of AD 297 from which this comes, see **S1.2** below.
Pius' second salutation as imperator in AD 142 (*ILS* 340) suggests that most of the campaigning was concluded under Lollius Urbicus. Coins of AD 143–4: *L4* 53. Building of Balmuidy fort: *L4* 55.
Distance slabs on Antonine Wall (all undated): *L4* 56–58.
The frontier in the 150s: *L4* 60–64.

L.   MARCUS AURELIUS (AD 161–180)

L1.1.   *(On his accession, AD 161)* War was also threatening in Britain, and the Chatti had invaded Germany and Raetia. Calpurnius Agricola was sent to deal with the Britons and Aufidius Victorinus with the Chatti.

[*Historia Augusta, Marcus* 8.7]

L1.2.   *(On the death of Lucius Verus, AD 169)* In addition, the Parthians and the Britons were on the verge of war.

[*Historia Augusta, Marcus* 22.1]

L1.3.   As their contribution to the alliance the Iazyges immediately provided Marcus with 8,000 cavalry, of which he sent 5,500 to Britain. *(AD 175)*

[Cassius Dio, *Roman History* 71.16.2]

Calpurnius Agricola: *HA, Marcus* 8.7–8. Building at Corbridge: *L4* 65. Altars: *L4* 66–67.

M.   COMMODUS (AD 177–192)

M1.   Ulpius Marcellus, governor *c.* AD 178–184

Commodus also had some wars with the barbarians beyond Dacia, in which Albinus and Niger, both of whom later fought against the emperor Severus, distinguished themselves; but his greatest war was in Britain. The tribes in the island crossed the wall that separated them from the Roman legions, did a great deal of damage, and cut down a general and his troops, so Commodus in alarm sent Ulpius Marcellus against them. Marcellus, who was a temperate and frugal man and who organised his diet and the rest of his life on military lines when he was on campaign, was becoming haughty and arrogant; he was obviously quite incorruptible but at the same time was not at all an engaging or friendly personality... Marcellus inflicted a major defeat on the barbarians and, when he was subsequently on the point of being put to death by Commodus for showing individual qualities, he was spared.

[Cassius Dio, *Roman History* 72.8.1]

Ulpius Marcellus: Altar: *L4* 69. Aqueduct to Chesters fort: *L4* 70. Coins: *L4* 71.

M2.   Unrest in Britain, *c.* AD 185/6

M2.1.   [6.1] At this time the successes achieved in Sarmatia by other generals were attributed by Perennis to his own son. [2] This Perennis, however, who enjoyed such power, had relieved generals of senatorial rank of their command in the British war and replaced them with equestrians. This was reported by the army's legates and Perennis was suddenly declared to be an enemy of the state, and handed over to the soldiers to be torn to pieces. Commodus replaced him in his position of power with Cleander, a chamberlain.

[*Historia Augusta, Commodus* 6.1–2]

M2.2. Commodus was also called Britannicus by his flatterers, although the Britons actually wanted to choose an emperor to oppose him.

[Historia Augusta, Commodus 8.4]

M2.3. The soldiers in Britain chose Priscus, a legate, as emperor but he declined, saying that he was no more an emperor than they were soldiers.

[Cassius Dio, Roman History 72.9.2ª]

M2.4. The officers in Britain, therefore, having been reprimanded for their plotting – they did not settle down until Pertinax quelled them – chose from their number 1,500 javelin-men and sent them to Italy. Nobody tried to stop them and when they were approaching Rome Commodus met them and asked: "Fellow-soldiers, what is this? What request do you bring?" "We have come," they said, "because Perennis is plotting against you with a view to making his son emperor." Commodus believed them, especially since they were supported by Cleander, all of whose plans had been thwarted by Perennis and who consequently loathed him.

[Cassius Dio, Roman History 72.9.2²]

Perennis had been sole commander of the Praetorian Guard since a plot against Commodus in AD 182. In 185 or 186 he was killed by mutinous troops in unclear circumstances involving a detachment from Britain (accounts differ). Cleander was an imperial freedman.

M3.   Pertinax

M3.1. He won promotion by his vigorous service in the Parthian war and was transferred to Britain, where he was retained.

[Historia Augusta, Pertinax 2.1]

M3.2. When Perennis had been put to death Commodus made amends to Pertinax and requested him by letter to set out for Britain. When he had done so he deterred the soldiers from any rebellion, although they wanted to set up someone, preferably Pertinax himself, as their emperor. Then Pertinax acquired a reputation for vindictiveness, because he was said to have laid charges before Commodus that Antistius Burrus and Arrius Antoninus were aspiring to the throne. And in fact he did personally put down a rebellion against himself in Britain, but he came into great danger and was almost killed in the mutiny of a legion, and was definitely left among the dead. Pertinax punished this uprising with great severity. Then later he asked to be excused from his position as legate, saying that his maintenance of discipline had made the legions hostile to him.

[Historia Augusta, Pertinax 3.5–10]

After two junior posts in Britain, Pertinax returned as governor, *c.* AD 185–190, before becoming emperor for three months in AD 193.

SEVERUS AND THE THIRD CENTURY,
AD 193–284

N.   SEPTIMIUS SEVERUS (AD 193–211)

N1.   Severus' accession (AD 193) and the civil war

N1.1.   This is what happened in Rome, and I shall now describe external events and rebellions. At that time three men, each of whom commanded three legions of citizens as well as large numbers of foreigners, were aiming at power: they were Severus, (Gaius Pescennius) Niger and (Decimus Clodius) Albinus, the governors respectively of Pannonia, Syria and Britain.

[Cassius Dio, *Roman History* 73.14.3]

N1.2.   Of the three generals that I mentioned, Severus was the shrewdest; he had foreseen that after Julianus had been deposed the three of them would come into conflict and fight against each other for the Empire, and had determined to win over to his own side the one nearest to him. Accordingly he had sent a letter by trusted messenger to Albinus, appointing him Caesar; for he despaired of Niger, who was priding himself on being the choice of the people. So Albinus, imagining that he was going to share the rule with Severus, remained where he was; while Severus, having won over the whole of Europe except Byzantium, hurried to Rome.

[Cassius Dio, *Roman History* 73.15.1]

N1.3.   Before Severus had scarcely drawn breath after his foreign wars he was involved in another one, a civil war this time, against his Caesar, Albinus. Severus was no longer according him the rank of Caesar, now he had removed Niger, and had arranged matters generally in that part of the empire as he wanted them; whereas Albinus was looking for the pre-eminent position of emperor. *(AD 196)*

[Cassius Dio, *Roman History* 75.4.1]

N1.4.   When he heard that Severus was moving quickly and was on the point of arriving, Albinus, who was leading a life of inactivity and luxury, was thrown into considerable confusion. He crossed with an expeditionary force from Britain to the nearest part of Gaul and sent word to all the neighbouring provinces, telling the governors to send money and provisions for the army. Some obeyed and sent them – to their cost, for they paid the penalty in due course. Those who ignored his instructions made their decision more by good luck than good judgment and were safe. Their decision proved right or wrong according to how the war happened to go.

[Herodian, *History* 3.7.1]

N1.5.   Severus settled affairs in Britain and divided the authority there between two governors.

[Herodian, *History* 3.8.2]

The civil wars: Cassius Dio 75.6.1–8.4; Herodian 2.15.1–5: 3.5.1–7, 8; Orosius 7.17.1.
Coin of Albinus: *L4* 74.
Herodian may be mistaken in placing the division of Britain into two provinces at this point.

N2. Descriptions of Britain

N2.1. [3.14.6] Most of Britain is marshland, since it is flooded by the ocean tides. It is the custom of the barbarians to swim in these swamps, or to run in them submerged to the waist. Because the greater part of the body is naked they do not mind the mud. [7] They are unfamiliar with the use of clothing, but decorate their waists and necks with iron, valuing this metal as an ornament and as a symbol of wealth in the way that other barbarians value gold. They tattoo their bodies with various patterns and with pictures of all kinds of animals. This is why they do not wear clothes, so as not to cover up the pictures on their bodies. [8] They are fearsome and dangerous fighters, defended only by a narrow shield and a spear, with a sword slung from their naked bodies. They are unaccustomed to breastplates and helmets, believing them to be a hindrance in crossing the marshes. A thick mist rises from the marshes, so that the atmosphere in the country is always gloomy. It was for these conditions that Severus got ready what was suitable for the Roman army, and likely to damage or impede a barbarian attack.

[Herodian, *History* 3.14.6–8]

N2.2. [76.12.1] In Britain there are two very large nations, the Caledonians and the Maeatae, and the names of the others have become included in these. The Maeatae live by the wall which divides the country into two halves, and the Caledonians beyond them. They both inhabit wild and waterless mountains and lonely and swampy plains without walls, cities or cultivated land. They live by pasturing flocks, hunting, and off certain fruits; [2] for although the stocks of fish are limitless and immense, they leave them untouched. They live in tents, unclothed and unshod, sharing their women and bringing up all their children together. Their government is for the most part democratic, and because their especial pleasure is plundering, they choose the bravest men to be their rulers. [3] They fight both in chariots with small, quick horses, and on foot, when they run very fast and also stand their ground with great determination. Their arms are a shield, and a short spear with a bronze apple on the end of the shaft, which they can shake and make a din with to dismay the enemy, and they also have daggers. [4] They can endure hunger and cold and any form of hardship; for they plunge into the marshes and hold out for many days with only their heads above water, and in the forest they live off bark and roots; and for any crises they prepare a sort of food, and when they have eaten a portion of this the size of a bean they do not become hungry or thirsty.

[5] Such then is the island of Britain, and such its inhabitants, at any rate in the hostile part. For it is an island, and had then clearly been proved to be so, as I have said. Its length is 7,132 stades, and its breadth 2,310 at the widest point and 300 at the narrowest. Of this area we hold a little less than half.

[Cassius Dio, *Roman History* 76.12.1–5]

For earlier estimates of the size of Britain, see **A15** above. Dio's length is equivalent to around 1,320 km

/ 820 miles, and his breadths to 430 km / 270 miles and 55 km / 35 miles, as compared to present-day calculations of approximately 1,000 km / 600 miles north-south, and the narrowest breadth as 64 km / 40 miles at the Forth-Clyde isthmus, the site of the Antonine Wall.

N3.   Severus goes to Britain to put down a rebellion (*c.* AD 208)

N3.1.   The Caledonians instead of honouring their promises had prepared to defend the Maeatae, and Severus at that time was concentrating on the Parthian war; so Lupus had no choice but to buy peace from the Maeatae for a considerable sum of money, recovering a few captives. *(AD 197)*

[Cassius Dio, *Roman History* 75.5.4]

Virrius Lupus was governor *c.*197/8; see also *L4* 76–77.

N3.2.   When Severus was told of these various activities, he was angry that while other men were winning wars for him in Britain, he himself was losing to a brigand in Italy. *(AD 207)*

[Cassius Dio, *Roman History* 76.10.6]

Brigand: For over a year *c.*206/7 Bulla Felix with his band robbed the rich and freed slaves in rural Italy, until eventually he was caught by trick.

N3.3.   Severus, seeing that his sons were changing their way of life and that the armies were becoming slack through inactivity, undertook a campaign against Britain, although he knew he would not return. This knowledge came chiefly from the stars... and from what he was told by the seers ... He did not return but died in the third year after this. He took a great deal of money on the expedition. *(AD 208)*

[Cassius Dio, *Roman History* 76.11.1]

N3.4.   [3.14.1] Such was the life that his sons were leading. Severus was upset by this, and by their undignified enthusiasm for the public shows. This was the situation when a despatch arrived from the governor of Britain to the effect that there was a rebellion among the barbarians there. They were laying waste the country, plundering, and causing widespread destruction. The defence of the place required more troops or the emperor's presence. [2] This was welcome news for Severus, since in any case by nature he enjoyed winning renown, and after the victories and titles he had won in the east and north he wanted to raise trophies over the Britons as well; but another factor was that he wanted to take his sons out of Rome, so that they might come to their senses in the disciplined life of the army, away from the luxury of the capital. He therefore announced his expedition to Britain.

Although now an old man and afflicted with arthritis, his spirit was as strong as any young man's. [3] He persevered with the journey, although carried most of the way in a litter, and never stopped to rest for long. Together with his sons he covered the distance with astonishing speed, and sailing across the ocean he reached Britain; summoning troops from all directions he assembled a large army and made his preparations for the war.

[4] The unexpected arrival of the emperor, and the news of the great army which had been collected to deal with them, alarmed the Britons, and they sent delegates to discuss peace-terms and tried to offer an explanation for their offences. [5] Severus however wanted to prolong his time in Britain and not return hurriedly to Rome, and furthermore it was his ambition to add to his victories and titles by a campaign against the British, so he sent the delegates away empty-handed, and put everything in order for the war. In particular he attempted to divide up the marshy districts with causeways so that his men by running along them without difficulty could advance in safety and then have a firm footing on a secure platform while they were fighting.

[Herodian, *History* 3.14.1–5]

Severus named as co-emperors his elder son Antoninus (Caracalla) in AD 198 and his younger son Geta in AD 209. For the entire ruling family to be together and so far from Rome was unprecedented. *Profectio* ('setting out') coins of Antoninus: *L4* 93–95. Expeditionary force: *L4* 91, 96.

N3.5. [3.14.9] When Severus considered that preparations for the war were complete, he left the younger of his two sons, Geta, in the territory which was under Roman rule, to see to the judicial and civil aspects of government, with a council consisting of his own older friends, and he himself took Antoninus and made war on the barbarians. [10] The army crossed the rivers and earthworks on the frontier of the Roman Empire, and frequent battles and skirmishes took place in which the barbarians were put to flight. But the Britons escaped without difficulty and hid in the woods and marshes; they used their knowledge of the country, and all this told against the Romans and prolonged the war.

[Herodian, *History* 3.14.9–10]

N3.6. [76.13.1] Severus, therefore, who wanted to conquer the whole of the island, invaded Caledonia. As he crossed it he had untold trouble cutting down the forests, levelling the high ground, filling in the swamps, and bridging the rivers; [2] for he fought no battle and saw no enemy drawn up for battle. The enemy put out sheep and cattle which the soldiers went to seize and so, as the enemy intended, were lured on until they were worn out; they were caused great suffering by the waters, and when they scattered they came under attack. Then, when they were unable to walk, they were killed by their fellow-soldiers so that they would not be captured, and consequently as many as a full fifty thousand perished. [3] But Severus did not give up until he was close to the end of the island, and there, in particular, he observed most closely the change in the sun's course and the length of the days and nights in summer and winter. [4] After being thus carried through practically the whole of the enemy's country – he was literally carried for much of the way, in a sort of covered litter, because of his lack of strength, he forced the Britons to come to an agreement whereby they were to abandon a considerable part of their country, and returned to friendly territory. *(AD 209)*

[Cassius Dio, *Roman History* 76.13.1–4]

Victory dedications: *L4* 82, 87.

N3.7. Britain afforded Severus the opportunity of moving on to greater things. He drove back the enemy and fortified the country with a wall which ran across the island, terminating at the sea on either side.

[Aurelius Victor, *Caesars* 20.18]

N3.8. Severus waged his last war in Britain, and in order to secure thoroughly the provinces he had retrieved, he built a rampart 32 miles long from sea to sea.

[Eutropius, *Brief History* 8.19.1]

Rebuilding forts before and during Severus' campaigns: south of Hadrian's Wall: *L4* 76–79; along and north of the wall: *L4* 80, 83 85–86; in Wales: *L4* 89–90.
Later withdrawal to Hadrian's Wall: Cassius Dio 77.1.1; Herodian 3.15.6.
Further references crediting Severus with wall-building: *HA, Severus* 18.2; *Epitome of the Caesars* 20.4; Orosius 7.17.7–8; Jerome *Chronicle*, under AD 207.

N3.9. When there was rebellion in the island again, he summoned his soldiers and ordered them to invade the rebels' territory and kill everyone they met, and he used this quotation:

> Let no one escape utter destruction at our hands;
> Let not the infant still carried in its mother's womb,
> If it be male, escape from its fate. *(AD 211)*

[Cassius Dio, *Roman History* 76.15.1]

Quotation: Homer, *Iliad* 6.57–59 (ending changed).

N4.   Death of Severus

N4.1. He had inspected the wall and was returning to the nearest residence after not only winning the victory, but concluding a permanent peace. While he was wondering what sort of omen would present itself to him, an Ethiopian from a military unit came to meet him (and prophesied his death).

[*Historia Augusta, Severus* 22.4]

N4.2. Not much later Severus died of disease in Britain, in the township of which the name is York, in the eighteenth year of his reign. *(February AD 211)*

[Aurelius Victor, *Caesars* 20.27]

N4.3. He died in Britain at York, after conquering tribes that seemed to be threatening Britain, in the eighteenth year of his reign, killed in his old age by a most grave illness.

[*Historia Augusta, Severus* 19.1]

N4.4. His last words are said to have been: "When I took over the state, chaos reigned everywhere; I am leaving it at peace, even Britain. I am an old and lame man, but the empire which I am leaving my Antonini is a strong one, if they turn out good, though weak, should they prove bad."

[*Historia Augusta, Severus* 23.3]

N4.5. [76.15.2] When this had been done, and the Caledonians had joined the rebellion of the Maeatae, he prepared to make war on them in person; but while he was occupied with this his sickness carried him off on the fourth of February, with some assistance, they say, from Antoninus. At any rate, before his death Severus is reported to have spoken these words to his sons (I give the actual words without embellishment): "Agree with each other, make the soldiers rich, and ignore everyone else."

[3] After this his body, in full military dress, was placed on a funeral pyre; the soldiers and his sons wheeled round it as a mark of honour; those who had soldiers' awards with them threw them on; and his sons lit the fire. [4] Subsequently his bones were placed in an urn of purple stone, taken to Rome, and deposited in the tomb of the Antonines. There is a story that shortly before his death Severus sent for the urn and after feeling it said: "You will hold a man for whom the inhabited world was not large enough."

[Cassius Dio, *Roman History* 76.15.2–3]

N4.6. [3.15.1] Severus was an old man and his arthritis now spread and forced him to remain in his quarters. He tried to send out Antoninus to manage the campaign, but Antoninus was only mildly interested in dealing with the enemy, and tried instead to gain control of the army. He began to persuade all the soldiers to pay attention only to him, slandered his brother, and used every means to court sole rule. [2] He had no sympathy for his father, who seemed to be a nuisance, very ill as he was and taking a long time to die, and he tried to persuade the doctors and attendants to do the old man some harm while they were looking after him, so that he would be rid of him more quickly. But eventually Severus died anyway, and in pain, although it was mainly grief that killed him. [3] As far as war was concerned, he had achieved, in his lifetime, the most distinction of any of the emperors; no one before him had won so many victories against rivals in civil wars and barbarians in foreign wars. He died after a reign of eighteen years, with two youthful sons to succeed him, and he left them more money than had ever been left before, and an invincible army...

(3.15.4–5: How Antoninus killed the household attendants and doctors who had not helped him hasten his father's death, and how he tried to persuade the officers to make the army declare him sole emperor; but remembering how Severus had brought up them up as equals, the army remained loyal to both brothers.)

[6] Having no success in (bribing) the army, Antoninus came to terms with the barbarians and granted them peace in return for guarantees. He left the enemy's territory and now joined his brother and mother without delay. Upon this, their mother, the leading men and their father's friends and advisers tried to reconcile them. [7] Because they all opposed his wishes, Antoninus was forced by pressure rather than inclination into a partnership and friendship that was faked rather than genuine. So

they both managed the imperial business with equal rank. They decided to set sail from Britain and made for Rome, taking their father's remains ...

[8] Taking the army with them as if they themselves had triumphed over the Britons, they crossed the ocean and reached Gaul on the other side.

[Herodian, *History* 3.15.1–8]

O.   ANTONINUS (CARACALLA) (AD 198–217)

O1.1.   Twenty-three or, as some say, twenty-five legions of citizens were being maintained at this time [AD 5]. At present only nineteen of them still exist, as follows: the Second Augusta, with its headquarters in Upper Britain ... the two Sixth legions, of which one, called Victrix, is stationed in Lower Britain ... the Twentieth, called both Valeria and Victrix, stationed in Upper Britain. *(Perhaps written about AD 215)*

[Cassius Dio, *Roman History* 55.23.2–5]

O1.2.   After this Antoninus assumed complete control; in theory he ruled with his brother, but in practice he enjoyed sole rule from the start. He made treaties with the enemy, evacuated their territory, and abandoned the forts.

[Cassius Dio, *Roman History* 77.1.1]

Antoninus had Geta, his brother and co-emperor, murdered in late AD 211.
Declarations of loyalty to Caracalla: *L4* 98–99.
Rebuilding on the northern frontier under Caracalla: *L4* 100. Under Elagabalus: *L4* 102–107 (AD 220–5).
Under Gordian III: *L4* 109–112 (AD 238–44). Under Valerian and Gallienus: *L4* 113 (AD 253–7).

P.   POSTUMUS (AD 260–268)

P1.   In Gaul Postumus seized power. This in fact was beneficial to the state because for ten years he showed great virtue and moderation, driving out the enemy who had been in control and restoring his ruined provinces to their former appearance; but he was killed by a mutiny among his soldiers.

[Orosius, *History against the Pagans* 7.22.10]

After the Sassanian defeat and capture of the emperor Valerian in AD 260, emergency leaders took over in some regions of the empire. Postumus was recognised as emperor by several of the western provinces, including Gaul, Britain and Spain. This so-called 'Gallic Empire' was re-integrated with the Empire in AD 274. Military rebuilding: *L4* 114.

Q.   PROBUS (AD 276–282)

Q1.1.   Probus also put a stop to another rebellion, which broke out in Britain. He used Victorinus, a Moor by birth, whose advice he had followed when appointing to the British command the man who was now rebelling. Summoning Victorinus, he blamed his advice and sent him to put his mistake right. Victorinus at once set out for Britain and by a shrewd trick removed the usurper.

[Zosimus, *New History* 1.66.2]

Q1.2.   Probus fought in person against the Burgundi and the Vandals . . . Those whom he was able to get into his hands alive he sent to Britain; when they had found homes there they were useful to the emperor when anyone later rebelled.

[Zosimus, *New History* 1.68.1]

Burgundi and Vandals: Germanic tribes who were attacking on the Rhine and Danube frontiers respectively.

Carinus and Numerian took the title Britannicus Maximus (*ILS* 608), which suggests a victory in Britain c.283/4.

CARAUSIUS AND THE FOURTH CENTURY, AD 284–410

R.   CARAUSIUS (AD 287–293) and ALLECTUS (AD 293–296)

R1.1.   [9.21] At this time too Carausius, although of very humble birth, had achieved an outstanding reputation in a vigorous military career. He had been given the responsibility throughout the Belgic and Armorican areas, with his headquarters at Boulogne, of clearing the sea, which was infested by the Franks and Saxons. On many occasions he captured large numbers of barbarians but he failed either to return all the booty to the provincials or to send it to the Emperor, and a suspicion grew up that he was letting in the barbarians on purpose so that he could catch them as they passed with their booty and grow rich on the proceeds. So Maximianus ordered him to be put to death, whereupon he declared himself emperor and seized Britain.

[22] So there was turmoil everywhere. Carausius was rebelling in Britain, Achilleus in Egypt; the Quinquegentiani were stirring up trouble in Africa, and Marseus was making war on the East. Diocletian raised Maximianus Herculius from the rank of Caesar to that of Augustus, and made Constantius and Maximianus Caesars . . . But he eventually made peace with Carausius, after trying an unsuccessful war against this master of strategy. Carausius was killed seven years later by his colleague Allectus, who held Britain himself for three years before the commander of the Praetorian Guard, Asclepiodotus, took command and overpowered him. So Britain was recovered, after ten years.

[Eutropius, *Brief History* 9.21–22]

R1.2.   [39.40] After six years, Allectus removed Carausius by treachery. [41] Allectus had been appointed by him as his chief financial officer, but frightened at his own crimes and the consequent prospect of being put to death, he took the law into his own hands and seized power.

[Aurelius Victor, *Caesars* 39.40–41]

See also: Aurelius Victor, *Caesars* 39.19–21; Orosius 7.25.3; *L4* 115–117.

S.   CONSTANTIUS I (CHLORUS) (AD 293–306)

S1.   The defeat of Allectus and recovery of Britain (AD 296)

S1.1.   Without doubt Britain, although but a single name, was a land that the state could ill afford to lose, so plentiful are its harvests, so numerous are the pasturelands in which it rejoices, so many are the metals of which seams run through it, so much wealth comes from its taxes, so many ports encircle it, to such an immense area does it extend.

[*Panegyric of Constantius* 11.1]

From a speech made by an unknown Gallic orator in AD 297 in honour of Constantius I.

S1.2.   [12] In this outrageous act of brigandage the escaping pirate first of all seized the fleet which had previously been protecting Gaul, and added a large number of ships which he built to the Roman pattern. He took over a legion, intercepted some detachments of provincial troops, press-ganged Gallic tradesmen into service, lured over with spoils from the provinces themselves numerous foreign forces, and trained them all under the direction of the ringleaders of this conspiracy for naval duties; and your troops, although unrivalled in courage, were nonetheless inexperienced at sea. So we heard that from an abominable act of piracy a dire threat of war had arisen, confident though we might be of the outcome. For as the days passed and the rebellion went unpunished this too had increased the audacity of these reckless men; they were boasting about the unfavourable conditions at sea, which had delayed your victory with the inevitability of fate, as if you were terrified of them; and they were so confident that the war had been not deliberately postponed but abandoned in despair, that now an underling forgot that they were all to share the punishment, and slew the chief pirate; he imagined that to repay him thus for bringing them into such danger was to be a real ruler.

[13] This war, therefore, which was so pressing, so inaccessible, so long established, so organised, you, Caesar, undertook; and in such a way that no sooner had you directed the withering flame of your might upon it than all men deemed it finished. First of all – and this required especial care – you ensured by invoking the might of your father that while your power was directed towards that war the foreign nations should not attempt revolt. For you yourself, you, lord Maximianus, eternal Emperor, deigning with marvellous speed to hasten your godlike arrival, at once took up your stand upon the Rhine and guarded that frontier not with forces of cavalry or infantry, but by the terror of your presence. Maximianus was as powerful as any number of armies on the river bank. But you, invincible Caesar, drew up and armed separate fleets and rendered the enemy so confused and undecided that he then at last realised that he was not protected but imprisoned by the sea.

[14] At this point one recalls how gracious was the fortune, in the administration of the state and the winning of renown, that attended those Emperors who stayed at Rome to win their triumphs and take the names of races conquered by their generals. Thus Fronto, almost the most shining example of Roman eloquence, when he was giving Antoninus the credit for finishing the war in Britain, claimed that although the emperor stayed in his palace in Rome and delegated responsibility for the war, he deserved the glory for the whole start and progress of the expedition as though he had taken charge of the steering of a warship [= **K1.3** *above*]. But you, invincible Caesar, not only by virtue of your rule directed that whole voyage and war, but also encouraged and inspired it with your very presence and by the example of your steadfastness. For you led the way in setting sail from the coast of Boulogne upon the troubled waters of the ocean; and so you inspired your army, which had sailed down the river Seine, with such unquenchable ardour, that while generals still delayed, while wind and waves were turbulent, the army on their own accord demanded the signal for departure, scorned ominous portents which now appeared, and made sail on a rainy day using, since the wind was not straight astern, one which blew across their course. Who would not dare to commit himself to a sea, however rough, when you were sailing? They say that when the men heard that you had set sail, their shouting and encouragement were

unanimous: "Why are we hesitating? Why are we delaying? Our commander himself has already set sail, is now voyaging forward, has perhaps already arrived. Let us try anything, no matter how great the waves through which we go. What is there for us to fear? We follow Caesar."

[15] Nor did their trust in your fortune deceive them since, as I have heard from eye-witnesses' accounts, at that very moment such mists swirled across the face of the sea that the enemy fleet, which was stationed on the look-out and in ambush at the Isle of Wight, was passed with the enemy in total ignorance and without a chance even to delay the attack, little though they could have done to stop it. And again, what of the fact that that same army, invincible under your direction, set fire to its own ships as soon as it had landed on the British coast? What prompted that but the remembrance of your divinity? And what reasoning led them not to keep any camp to which to retreat, not to fear the uncertainties of the battlefield, not to imagine, so it is reported, that the fortunes of war were equally balanced, except that consideration of you led to a certainty that there could be no doubt of victory? It was not their strength, it was not their human resources that they had in mind then, but your divine power. Whatever sort of battle is in prospect, it is the good fortune of generals, more than the confidence of soldiers, that guarantees success. And the very standard-bearer of the impious plot – why did he leave the shore which he was holding? Why did he desert fleet and harbour? Unless, invincible Caesar, it was because he was afraid that you, whose sails he had seen in the offing, were on the very point of coming. He preferred by any means to test his fortune against your generals than to face in person the onslaught of your might. Poor fool, who did not realise that wherever he fled, the force of your divinity was present wherever your features and standards were venerated!

[16] Yet in his flight he fell into the hands of your soldiers; defeated by you, he was crushed by your armies. In fact so frightened was he, so often looking behind him for you, so dumbfounded like a witless fool, as he hurried to his death, that he did not set out his line of battle or draw up all the forces he was dragging with him; instead, forgetting all his preparations, he rushed into battle with the original authors of that conspiracy and detachments of foreign mercenaries. So, Caesar, did your good fortune render even this benefit to the state, that the Roman Empire prevailed with scarcely the death of a single Roman. I am told it was only the prostrate corpses of our foul enemy that covered those plains and hills. Then indeed those native corpses, or so they seemed from how they had been dressed and their luxuriant tawny hair, lay disfigured with dust and gore, scattered in all directions wherever the agony of wounds had led them; and among them was the very standard-bearer of brigandage, with the imperial robe that he had usurped in his lifetime deliberately laid aside, identified with difficulty on the evidence of a single garment. So truly had he taken counsel with himself on the approach of death, that he was reluctant to be recognised when dead.

[17] In very truth, invincible Caesar, so willingly have all the immortal gods granted that you should slaughter every enemy you attack, and especially the Franks, that your other soldiers, who had become separated and lost their way in the poor visibility at sea, as I have described, reached London and in every direction throughout the city destroyed what was left from the battle of that horde of foreign mercenaries, who

were planning to make good their escape after sacking the place. So to the inhabitants of your province they brought not only safety by the slaughter of the enemy but the pleasure too of witnessing it. What a manifold victory, won by so many triumphs! By it Britain was restored; the strength of the Franks utterly eradicated; the necessity of obedience imposed on many other tribes found guilty of complicity in that crime; and the seas cleared for a lasting security. You may boast, invincible Caesar, that you discovered another world; for in restoring naval renown to Rome's might you added to your empire an element greater than all lands. In a word, you have concluded, invincible Caesar, a war which seemed to threaten all provinces and could have spread and flared up over an area as wide as that which the whole ocean and gulfs of the inland seas wash with their waters.

[*Panegyric of Constantius* 12–17]

Defeat of Allectus: also Orosius 7.25.6; *L4* 118.
Military building: *L4* 118.

S1.3.   Amply deserved therefore was the triumphant rejoicing which spread itself in the path of your greatness from the moment that you, the avenger and liberator for whom men had prayed, at last put in at that shore. The overjoyed Britons came with their wives and children to meet you. They gazed upon you as though you had descended from the skies above; and it was not only you they worshipped, but even the sails and oars of the ship which had conveyed your divine presence; and they were ready to feel you walk over their prostrated bodies. No wonder that they were transported with such joy; for after so many years of the most wretched captivity, after the violation of their wives, after the degrading servitude of their children, now at last they were free; now at last they were Roman; now at last they were revived by the true light of our rule.

[*Panegyric of Constantius* 19]

S1.4.   [5.1] Who is there who does not, I will not say remember, but rather still see how Constantius extended and embellished the empire? [2] As soon as he was called to the throne, he cut off the port from the Ocean, afloat with the innumerable ships of the enemy fleet, blockading by land and sea the army which occupied the shore of Boulogne. For he threw a mole across the tides of the sea, so that for those whose gates had been washed by the waves, contact with the sea, near as it was, was cut off. [3] The army which he had conquered by his virtue he preserved by his clemency. He prepared for the recovery of Britain by building a fleet. Meanwhile he swept every enemy from the land of Batavia, which had been occupied by various Frankish tribes under one who had actually been, at one time, a protégé of his. Not content with conquering the Franks he made them settle on Roman land, so that they were forced not only to lay down their arms but to abandon their savage character.

[4] What shall I say of the recovery of Britain? His voyage there was over so quiet a sea that Ocean itself, as if stupefied by such a traveller, seemed to lose all natural movement. His journey was such that Victory rather waited for him to land than accompanied him.

[*Panegyric of Constantine* 5.1–4]

From a speech made by an unknown Gallic orator in AD 310 in honour of the emperor Constantine I, son of Constantius I, to celebrate his *quinquennalia* (five years in power).

S1.5.   The day would not be long enough for my oration, if I were to recount, however briefly, all of your father's deeds. In that last great expedition of his he did not seek, as is popularly believed, merely British trophies; when the gods were already calling him, he attained the farthest limit of the earth. So many and such great things were achieved. But he did not seek to occupy the forests and swamps of the Caledonians and other Picts, nor neighbouring Ireland or far-distant Thule, nor yet the Fortunate Isles, if such there be. Although he was unwilling to speak of this with any man, he, who was about to join the gods, went to contemplate Ocean, the Progenitor of gods, bathed in the light of the fiery star of heaven. Thus he who was about to enjoy perpetual light foresaw this in the nearly continuous day.

[*Panegyric of Constantine* 7.1]

For the earliest reference to the Picts, in a speech of AD 297, see **A13.5** above.

S2.   The death of Constantius at York and accession of Constantine I

S2.1   When Constantius died, all of those present bent their efforts to make Constantine emperor, but especially Crocus, the King of the Alamanni, who attended Constantius as one of his chief supporters.

[*Epitome of the Caesars* 41.3]

Epitome of the Caesars: brief biographies of the Emperors from Augustus to Theodosius I, written in the late 4th century (author unknown).

S2.2.   Then Galerius sent Constantine back to his father. In order to avoid Severus while travelling through Italy, Constantine crossed the Alps with the greatest speed, and maimed the post-horses which he left behind him. He reached his father at Boulogne (for which the Gallic name used to be Gesoriacum). But after defeating the Picts his father Constantius died at York, and by the unanimous decision of his troops Constantine became Caesar.

[Anonymus Valesianus 2.4]

The Severus referred to here is Severus II, AD 306–7.
Constantine may have taken the title Britannicus Maximus for this campaign (*ILS* 8942); see also Eusebius *Life of Constantine* 1.8.
Anonymus Valesianus: a late 4th-century biography of Constantine (author unknown).

T.   CONSTANTINE I (AD 306–337)

T1.   British bishops at the Council of Arles, AD 314

Eborius bishop of the city of York in the province of Britain.
Restitutus bishop of the city of London in the above-mentioned province.
Adelphius bishop of the city of the Colony *[Lincoln?]*.

Also Sacerdos priest and Arminius deacon.

[*Council of Arles* (Mansi II 476)]

This was the first church council called by imperial command; its minutes include a list of those attending.

T2.   Britain in the Verona List

T2.1.   The Diocese of the Britains has four provinces:
1 (Britannia) Prima
2 (Britannia) Secunda
3 Maxima Caesariensis
4 Flavia Caesariensis

[*Verona List* 7]

The Verona List is a 7th-century copy of a list of the provinces of the Roman Empire originally drafted in the early 4th century. It records the twelve 'dioceses' (each under a 'Vicar') into which Diocletian had divided the Empire, and the hundred or so new smaller provinces he had created (each under a 'Prefect').

T2.2.   Barbarian peoples who have flourished under the emperors:
2 Scoti
3 Picti
4 Calidoni

[*Verona List* 13.1]

U.   CONSTANS I (AD 337–350)

U1.   Expedition to Britain, AD 343

You, most worshipful emperor, have extended your rule, and so that the greater glory may be shed upon your virtues, you have changed and scorned the order of the seasons by riding haughtily in winter across the swelling raging waves of Ocean, a deed not done before or destined to be done again. The waters of a sea still scarcely known to us before trembled beneath your oars, and the Briton quailed before the face of an unexpected emperor. What more do you desire? The very elements have yielded the victory to your virtues.

[Firmicus Maternus, *On the Errors of Profane Religions* 28.6]

An edict of Constans cited in the Theodosian Code (11.16.5) shows that he was at Boulogne on 25 January 343, presumably before crossing to Britain.
Firmicius Maternus was an astrologer turned Christian, who issued this appeal to Constans to eradicate pagan religion.

U2.   Gratian the Elder

The elder Gratian [*father of Valentinian I and Valens*], therefore, who was quite famous for his physical strength and stamina and his skill at wrestling in the military style, after holding the rank of member of the bodyguard and tribune, became a Count (*comes*) and took command of the army in Africa. There he was involved in suspected theft, and departed; and a considerable time afterwards he commanded the British army with the same rank. Eventually he returned home with an honourable discharge. (*Before* AD *350*)

[Ammianus Marcellinus, *History* 30.7.3]

V.   CONSTANTIUS II (AD 337–361)

V.1.   The aftermath of Magnentius' defeat

[14.5.6] Prominent among these was the secretary Paulus, a Spaniard, whose features masked a serpentine character, and who was very clever at sniffing out men's secret vulnerable points. He was sent to Britain to fetch some men in the army who had dared to join Magnentius' conspiracy, and since they could not offer any resistance he freely exceeded his instructions and suddenly undermined the fortunes of a large number of people, sweeping on like a flood with manifold devastation and ruin. Freeborn men were thrown into prison, and some crushed with manacles; many charges of course were fabricated and had no connection with the truth; and all this gave rise to an infamous crime which branded Constantius' time with an ineradicable mark. (AD *353/4*)

[7] Martinus, who was governing those provinces as Vicar of the Prefects, deplored the troubles inflicted upon innocent men and repeatedly pleaded that those who were innocent of any crime should be spared; and when his pleas were ignored he threatened to resign. He thought that the evil bloodhound would at any rate take fright at that and at last stop thrusting men who were living harmoniously into obvious danger.

[8] Paulus considered this a restriction on his activities; and, being a formidable artist in causing confusion – he had for this reason earned the nickname 'the Chain' – he drew the Vicar who was still defending those whom he governed into the fate that threatened them all. He even threatened to take him, as well as the tribunes and many others, in chains to the emperor's court. Martinus was moved by this and the threat of sudden destruction to attack Paulus with a sword. His hand was weak and having failed to strike a fatal blow he thrust the drawn sword into his own side. And so, by this ignominious death, died a most just ruler, who had dared to alleviate the pitiable misfortunes of many men.

[9] This was how Paulus carried out his crimes, and he returned to the Emperor's quarters steeped in blood, bringing crowds of men almost swathed in chains and in the deepest squalor and despair. Upon their arrival the racks were made ready and the executioner prepared his hooks and instruments of torture. Of these men many were proscribed, others exiled, and a number executed with the sword. No one readily recalls any man who was acquitted in the reign of Constantius, once such charges had reached the level of a whisper.

[Ammianus Marcellinus, *History* 14.5.6–9]

Magnentius, a Gaul who may have had a British father, was declared emperor by the army in 350, shortly before the death of Constans. He was recognised in Britain and held power until his suicide in AD 353.

For Vicar and Prefects, see the note to **T2.1** above.

V2.   Julian and grain from Britain (AD 358–359)

V2.1.   [279D] In the second and third years after this, all the barbarians had been driven out of Gaul, most of the cities had been recovered and a complete fleet of many ships had arrived from Britain. [280A] I had got together a fleet of 600 ships, 400 of which had been built in less than ten months, bringing them all together into the Rhine. This was no small achievement since the neighbouring barbarians kept attacking me. It had seemed so impossible to Florentius that he had agreed to pay the barbarians a fee of 2,000lbs of silver in return for a safe passage. Constantius learnt this, for Florentius wrote to tell him about it.

[280B] Constantius wrote to me, ordering me to carry out the agreement, unless I thought it altogether shameful. But how could it not be shameful, when it seemed so even to Constantius, who was always ready to try to conciliate barbarians? No payment was made to them. On the contrary I marched against them, and since the gods gave me their ready protection, I received the submission of part of the Salii and drove out the Chamavii, capturing many cattle and women and children. I terrified them to such an extent that they trembled at my approach. [280C] I at once received hostages from them, and thus secured a safe passage for my food supplies [*i.e. from Britain*].

[Julian, *Letter to the Senate and People of Athens* 279D–280C]

Julian, the nephew of Constantine I, was made Caesar in charge of Gaul and Britain by Constantius II in November 355; he became Emperor 361–363.

V2.2.   (The Chamavi sued for peace from Julian) . . . When Julian saw that peace with them would be not only opportune but indeed necessary, for the Chamavi could prevent supplies from Britain reaching the Roman garrisons, he made peace, demanding hostages as a guarantee of good faith.

[Eunapius, *fragment 12*]

Eunapius in the early 5th century wrote a history (in Greek) of the period 270–404, of which only some quotations by later authors survive; Zosimus (see List of Sources) also drew on Eunapius.

V2.3.   Julian himself, as it was the appropriate season, summoned his troops from all directions for a campaign, and set out; but before the heat of the battle he considered one of the most urgent tasks for him to carry out quickly was to enter those cities which had long since been laid in ruins and abandoned, and to restore and fortify them. He also replaced burnt-out granaries with new ones, so that they could house the corn which was regularly shipped from Britain. *(AD 359)*

[Ammianus Marcellinus, *History* 18.2.3]

See also Zosimus 3.5.2

V3. Synod of AD 359

*(A general synod was summoned and over 400 bishops from the West met at Rimini;
the Emperor ordered that they be given grants towards their expenses.)* But the
bishops from my own country, Aquitaine, and from Gaul and Britain thought that
this was improper: they rejected the grants and chose to live at their own expense.
Only three bishops from Britain were too poor not to use public funds; they had been
offered money collected among the others but they turned this down in the belief that
it was more pious to be a burden on the treasury than on individuals. I have heard that
my fellow-countryman Bishop Gavidius used to refer critically to this, but my own
opinion would have been quite different: I think it was to the bishops' credit that they
were so poor that they had nothing of their own, and by not accepting help from other
individuals in preference to the treasury they were not a burden to anyone.

[Sulpicius Severus, *Chronicle* 2.41]

Sulpicius Severus, a Gaul of the early 5th century, wrote a brief Christian summary of universal history to
AD 400.

V4. Rebellion in Britain, AD 360

[20.1.1] In the tenth consulship of Constantius and the third of Julian, the savage tribes
of the Scots and Picts were carrying out raids in Britain, having disrupted the agreed
peace, and laying waste places near the frontiers. Fear hung over the provinces, which
were already worn out with the accumulated disasters of previous years. Julian was
spending the winter in Paris and already had a variety of cares to occupy him; he was
afraid to cross the sea to help – as I said earlier that Constans did – because that would
have meant leaving Gaul without a ruler, and the Alamanni were already prepared
for a savage war. [2] He therefore decided that Lupicinus, at that time master of the
soldiers, should go and use either reason or force to settle the argument. He was, it
is true, a warlike man and skilled in military affairs, but one ... in whom men long
wondered whether avarice or cruelty prevailed.

[3] Taking therefore the light-armed auxiliaries, that is the Heruli and Batavi, and two
units derived from Moesia, this general in the dead of winter came to Boulogne, where
after obtaining ships and embarking all his troops he waited for a favourable wind. He
then sailed to Richborough on the opposite shore, and went on to London, intending
there to form plans according to the state of affairs that he found, and to hasten thence
quickly to the field of operations.

[Ammianus Marcellinus, *History* 20.1.1–3]

Ammianus never resumed the story of the campaigns of Lupicinus.

W.   VALENTINIAN I (AD 364–375) & VALENS (AD 364–378)

W1.   Barbarian attacks

At that time [*start of reign*, AD 364] it was as if the trumpets were sounding the signal for the battle throughout the entire Roman world. The most savage nations rose and poured across the nearest frontiers. Simultaneously the Alamanni were plundering Gaul and Raetia, the Sarmatae and Quadi were attacking Pannonia, and the Picts, Saxons, Scots and Attacotti harassed Britain in a never-ending series of disasters . . .

[Ammianus Marcellinus, *History* 26.4.5]

See also Ammianus Marcellinus 30.7.9–10.

W2.   Count Theodosius saves Britain, AD 367

W2.1.   [27.8.1] Valentinian therefore was marching quickly from Amiens to Trier when serious and alarming news reached him to the effect that a conspiracy of the barbarians had brought Britain to her knees. Count Nectaridus, officer responsible for coastal defences, had been killed, and the general Fullofaudes had been circumvented by the enemy.

[2] Horrified by such news, Valentinian sent Severus, who at that time still commanded the household troops, to retrieve the situation, if chance should present him with the necessary opportunity; but it was not long before he was recalled, and when Jovinus set out for the same area he allowed him to effect a rapid withdrawal, having decided to try for the support of a strong army, and maintaining that that was what the urgency of the situation demanded.

[3] According to persistent rumours which kept arriving about that island, many alarming developments were taking place, and eventually Theodosius was selected and told to go there as quickly as possible. His reputation was based on a very successful military career, and his fame, and confidence in him, preceded him as he hurried to depart after collecting an army of young and spirited legionary and auxiliary troops.

[4] I have already described to the best of my ability, when dealing with the emperor Constans, the tides and situation of Britain, and I do not consider it necessary to repeat the description – just as Homer's Ulysses shrinks from repeating his story to the Phaeacians; the task is too much. [5] The following details will suffice: the Picts at that time were divided into two tribes, the Dicalydonae and the Verturiones; there were also the Attacotti, a belligerent tribe, and the Scots, who ranged far and wide and caused great devastation. The areas facing Gaul were harassed by the Franks and their neighbours the Saxons; they broke out wherever they could, by land or sea, plundering and burning ruthlessly, and killing all their prisoners.

[6] So this most competent general set out for the remotest parts of the earth, to check these inroads if better luck should give him the opportunity, and he reached the coast at Boulogne. The narrow stretch of water which separates this coast from the lands

opposite alternately rises in terrifying tides and, without harming those who sail on it, becomes as level again as a plain. From Boulogne Theodosius crossed the straits unhurriedly and landed at Richborough, a quiet place opposite. [7] The Batavi, Heruli, Jovii and Victores followed, all units with high morale, and when they arrived, Theodosius made for London, the old town, called Augusta in more recent times. Subdividing his forces into many separate groups, he attacked the marauding bands of the enemy who were loaded down with plunder, quickly put to flight those who were driving along prisoners and cattle, and seized the booty taken from the wretched subject population. [8] This he restored to its owners, all except for a small part which was made over to his weary soldiers. Up to now the city had been overwhelmed by the greatest hardships, but suddenly, before rescue could have been expected, it was restored; and he entered it in triumph, like the hero of an ovation.

[9] Theodosius was encouraged by his excellent success to embark on a larger campaign, and he delayed in order to consider which plans were safe. He was undecided about his future course of action, having learned from the statements of captives and information brought by deserters that the enemy was a widely scattered one consisting of different tribes; they were indescribably wild and could only be defeated by greater cunning and unexpected attacks. [10] Eventually he published an edict in which he summoned deserters back to the ranks without penalty, together with the many others who had scattered in all directions on leave. This proclamation brought in large numbers of men who were encouraged by his offer. Now able to breathe again, he requested that Civilis and Dulcitius should be sent to him. Civilis, who had a rather fierce temper, but was dependably just and honourable, was to have in Britain the status of deputy prefect; Dulcitius was a general of outstanding military skill.

[Ammianus Marcellinus, *History* 27.8.1–10]

W2.2. [28.3.1] But Theodosius, a general with a fine reputation, had now made up his mind for action. Setting out from Augusta, formerly London, with an army he had gathered by intelligent hard work, he rendered the greatest assistance to the Britons, who had suffered misfortune and chaos. He reached first places everywhere that were suitable for ambushing the natives; and he demanded nothing of his ordinary soldiers in which he was not prepared instantly to take the lead himself. [2] In this way, combining the physical exertions of a common soldier with the responsibilities of a distinguished general, he defeated various tribes and put them to flight. An over-confidence encouraged by their apparent safety had inspired them to attack Roman property; but Theodosius completely restored the cities and forts which had suffered numerous disasters, although founded to create a long period of peace.

[3] While he was occupied in this way a very serious crime was committed, which would have posed a considerable threat if the enterprise had not been nipped in the bud. [4] A certain Valentinus, who was a native of Valeria in Pannonia, a proud man, whose sister was the wife of the pernicious Vicar Maximinus, later Praetorian Prefect, had been exiled to Britain for a serious offence. Like some dangerous animal he could not stay quiet; he pushed ahead with his destructive, revolutionary plans, nourishing an especial loathing for Theodosius who, as he saw, was the only man who could stand in

the way of his wicked designs. [5] However, he was exploring many possibilities both secretly and openly, and as his immoderate ambition became increasingly swollen, he approached exiles and soldiers, and promised them, as opportunity allowed, alluring rewards for the rash adventures he proposed.

[6] The time for effecting his plans was close; but the general Theodosius had heard of them from a source which he had arranged. Eager for action, determined with high purpose to punish the plot he had uncovered, he handed over Valentinus, and a few others who formed his immediate circle, to Dulcitius for capital punishment; but drawing on the military experience in which he was pre-eminent among his contemporaries, and looking to the future, he forbade investigations into the conspiracy to be pursued: he wanted to prevent fear spreading, and the troubles in the provinces which he had lulled to rest being brought to life again.

[7] So he totally removed this threat, and from this he turned to many other pressing reforms. It was widely acknowledged that good fortune never deserted him. He restored cities and the garrison's fortresses, as I have said, and protected the frontiers with sentries and forts. A province which he recovered had been in the enemy's power, and he restored it so well to its former condition as to give it – to quote his own report – a constitutional ruler; and henceforth, at the emperor's wish, it was called Valentia, because the emperor was as pleased at this vital news as if he were celebrating his own victory.

[8] During these outstanding events the *areani*, who had gradually become corrupt, were removed by him from their positions. This was an organisation founded in early times, of which I have already said something in the history of Constans. It was clearly proved against them that they had been bribed with quantities of plunder, or promises of it, to reveal to the enemy from time to time what was happening on our side. Their official duty was to range backwards and forwards over long distances with information for our generals about disturbances among neighbouring nations.

[9] After dealing so brilliantly with the affairs I have mentioned, and others like them, he left the provinces in a state of exaltation by the time he was summoned to the court. He had, by a series of salutary victories, won as much fame as Furius Camillus or Papirius Cursor. Accompanied by the good wishes of everyone he was escorted down to the water's edge, crossed with a gentle wind, and reached the imperial staff headquarters. He was received with joy and compliments, and Jovinus, for not showing initiative, lost to him the command of the cavalry.

[Ammianus Marcellinus, *History* 28.3.1–9]

Furius Camillus and Papirius Cursor: famous ancient Roman generals of the 4th century BC.

W2.3.   The moment has come to speak of the virtues of your father. But what shall I do? The wealth of topics makes my task unusually hard . . . Shall I tell of how Britain was crushed by battles on land? Then I shall be thinking of how the Saxon was exhausted by battles at sea. Shall I relate how the Scot was driven back to his marshes?

[*Panegyric of Theodosius I* 5.1]

From a speech made by Pacatus in AD 389 to the emperor Theodosius I, son of Count Theodosius, to celebrate the defeat of Magnus Maximus (see **X2** below).

W2.4. From Spain came Honorius' grandfather, for whom, while still exultant after his northern battles, Africa wove new laurels won from the Massyli. He pitched camp amidst the Caledonian frosts and endured in his helmet the midsummer heat of Libya, terrifying the Moor and conquering the British coast, devastating north and south alike. What help to the British is the unremitting harshness, the freezing cold, of their climate? What help their unknown waters? The Orcades were drenched with the slaughter of the Saxon; Thule became warm with Pictish blood; and icy Ireland wept over the burial-mounds of Scots.

[Claudian, *On the Fourth Consulship of Honorius* 23–34]

See also Claudian, *On the Third Consulship of Honorius* 54–58.

W2.5. Valentinian appointed Fraomarius king of the Bucinobantes, a tribe of the Alamanni opposite Mainz; but a little later, because a recent invasion had completely devastated that district, he transferred him to Britain with the rank of tribune and the command of what was then a large and strong force of Alamanni. *(AD 372)*

[Ammianus Marcellinus, *History* 29.4.7]

X. GRATIAN (AD 375–383) and THEODOSIUS I (AD 379–395)

X1. Attacks on Britain, AD 382

Maximus conducted a vigorous campaign, in which he defeated the Picts and Scots, who had carried out an invasion.

[Chronicler of 452, under 382]

From a Chronicle (in Latin) of the years 379–452 written by an unknown author, apparently in Gaul.

X2. The revolt of Maximus

X2.1. [4.35.2] Meanwhile Gratian was faced by a crisis which could not be taken lightly. Following the advice of those courtiers who make a habit of leading emperors astray he received some Alanian deserters, enrolled them in his armies, heaped presents upon them and considered them so highly as to entrust to them affairs of the greatest importance while disregarding his soldiers. [3] This engendered a hatred of the emperor among the soldiers, which quickly smouldered and grew and made them eager to rebel, especially those stationed in Britain, who were more stubborn and quick to take offence than the others. They were encouraged in this by Maximus, a native of Spain, who had served with the emperor Theodosius in Britain. [4] He was offended because Theodosius had been considered worthy to rule while he himself had not been promoted even to a post of dignity; and so he fostered the soldiers' hatred of the emperor. They readily rebelled, and named Maximus emperor; presenting him with the purple robe and diadem, they sailed across the sea without delay and put in at the mouths of the Rhine. *(AD 383)*

[Zosimus, *New History* 4.35.2-4]

Zosimus confuses the emperor Theodosius I with his father, Count Theodosius.

X2.2.   Theodosius subdued the foreign tribes in the east, freed Thrace at last from the enemy, and made his son Arcadius his colleague in power; but Maximus, an active and honourable man who deserved the rank of Augustus but for his defying his sacred oath and assuming illegal power, was made emperor almost against his will by the army in Britain, and crossed to Gaul. There he terrified the Augustus Gratian by his sudden invasion and while Gratian was considering crossing to Italy he ensnared and killed him; and he drove his brother, the Augustus Valentinian, from Italy.

[Orosius, *History against the Pagans* 7.34.9]

X2.3.   Associated with the larger fast warships are scouting vessels, with twenty oarsmen on either side. These the Britons call 'pictae' [*painted ships*]. They are intended to take the enemy by surprise, both by intercepting their supply ships, and also by observing their movements and discovering their plans. Since if brightly coloured they would be too easily seen, the sails and rigging of the scouting vessels are painted sea-green, the pitch which covers the hulls likewise. Even the sailors and soldiers are dressed in green, so that not only by night but also by day they become less visible when scouting.

[Vegetius, *Summary of Military Affairs* 4.37]

See *L4* 122 for signal stations in Britain.
Vegetius' military manual (in Latin) was probably written in the late 4th, or possibly the early 5th century AD.

Y.   HONORIUS (AD 395–423)

Y1.   Stilicho campaigns in Britain AD 400 – 401/2

Y1.1.   Next spoke Britannia, veiled with the skin of a wild beast of Caledonia, her cheeks tattooed, her blue cloak sweeping over her footprints like the surge of Ocean: "I too," she said, "when neighbouring tribes were destroying me – I too was fortified by Stilicho, when the Scot set all Ireland astir, and Tethys frothed with the enemy's oars. His was the care which ensured I should not fear the spears of the Scot, nor tremble at the Pict, nor watch all along my shore for the arrival of the Saxon with the shifting winds." *(AD 400)*

[Claudian, *On the Consulship of Stilicho* 2.247–255]

Y1.2.   And when our soldiers heard the news – such affection for their leader inspires them – they assembled with hurrying standards from every region, and at the

sight of Stilicho took heart again, with mingled sobs and tears of joy . . . The legion
came too which was set to guard the furthest Britons, which curbs the fierce Scot and
while slaughtering the Pict scans the devices tattooed on his lifeless form. *(AD 401/2)*

[Claudian, *On the Gothic War* 404–418]

For war against the Picts (AD 398?), see also Claudian, *First Poem against Eutropius* 391–3 (delivered spring
AD 399).

Y2.   The usurper Gratian (AD 407)

Y2.1.   While these tribes were rampaging through Gaul, in Britain Gratian, a citizen
of that island, was made tyrant and killed. Constantine, who had come from the lowest
ranks of the army, was elected in his place, solely on account of the confidence inspired
by his name and not because of any brave service. As soon as he assumed power he
crossed to Gaul.

[Orosius, *History against the Pagans* 7.40.4]

Constantine (also in Y2.2) is the western emperor Constantine III, AD 407 – 411. See also Zosimus 5.27.

Y2.2.   [6.2.1] While Arcadius was still emperor, and Honorius and Theodosius were
holding their seventh and second consulships respectively, the soldiers in Britain
rebelled and made Marcus emperor, obeying him as though he were the ruler of that
area. But he did not suit their ways and so they killed him and promoted Gratian. They
awarded him the purple robe and crown and gave him a bodyguard as though he were
emperor. [2] But not finding him to their liking either, after four months they deposed
and killed him and handed imperial rule to Constantine. He appointed Justinian and
Neviogastes to command the troops in the land of the Celts and crossed the sea, leaving
Britain; arriving at Boulogne, the nearest coastal town, a city of Lower Germany, he
spent some days there, and after he had won over all the troops on the frontier between
Gaul and Italy as far as the Alps his position as emperor seemed secure.

[Zosimus, *New History*, 6.2.1–2]

Y3.   Gerontius rebels against Constantine III (AD 409)

[6.5.2] Constans was again sent to Spain by his father, and he took the general Justus
with him. Gerontius took offence at this, and after winning over the troops of those
regions he succeeded in making the barbarians in the Celtic lands rebel against
Constantine. Constantine did not oppose them because the greater part of his forces
was in Spain; and the barbarians from across the Rhine, who now attacked in force,
reduced the inhabitants of Britain and some of the Celtic tribes to the point of throwing
off Roman rule and living independently, without further submission to Roman laws.
[3] So the Britons took up arms and facing danger for their own safety they freed
their cities from the barbarians who threatened them; and all Armorica and the other
provinces of Gaul followed the British example and freed themselves in the same way,
expelling their Roman governors and setting up their own administrations as best they
could. *(AD 409)*

[Zosimus, *New History*, 6.5.2–3]

Constans: Constans II (AD 409–11), son of the western emperor Constantine III. Gerontius installed Maximus as emperor. Both Gerontius and Maximus died in AD 411.

Y4.   Britain is abandoned, AD 410(?)

Y4.1.   Honorius sent letters to the British cities, telling them to look after their own defence.

[Zosimus, *New History* 6.10.2]

Some scholars suspect there a scribal error, and that Honorius' letter was addressed to the cities of Bruttium in southern Italy.

Y4.2.   The army of the Visigoths under Adaulphus marched on Gaul, and Constantine was defeated in battle and died with his sons. Nonetheless, the Romans were no longer able to recover Britain, which from that time continued to be ruled by those who seized power. *(AD 411)*

[Procopius, *Vandal War* 1.2.37–38]

See also Chronicler of 452, under AD 410.
Procopius was an officer and official under the emperor Justinian (mid-6th century) who wrote a history of Justinian's wars.

Z.   NOTITIA DIGNITATUM (Western section)

Z1.   Civilian officials

Z1.1.   Chapter 23, The Vicar of the Britains:
[8] Under the control of the *vir spectabilis*, the Vicar of the Britains:
[9]   Governors with the rank of *consularis*:
[10]   Maxima Caesariensis
[11]   Valentia
[12]   Governors with the rank of *praeses*:
[13]   Britannia Prima
[14]   Britannia Secunda
[15]   Flavia Caesariensis
            (*[16–26] list the administrative staff of the Vicar*)

Z1.2.   Chapter 11, The Count of the Sacred Largesses:
[20]   Rationalis of the Finances of the Britains
[37]   Praepositus of the Treasuries at Augusta [*London*] in the Britains
[60]   Procurator of the Weaving Factory in the Britains at Venta [*Winchester*]

Z1.3.   Chapter 12, The Count of the Private Property:
[15]   Rationalis of the Private Property in the Britains

Z2.   Military commanders and units

Z2.1.   Chapter 40, the Duke (*dux*) of the Britains:

[17] Under the control of the *vir spectabilis*, the Duke of the Britains:

[18]   Prefect of the Sixth Legion

[19]   Prefect of the Dalmatian Cavalry, at Praesidium [*uncertain*]

[20]   Prefect of the Crispian Cavalry, at Danum [*Doncaster*]

[21]   Prefect of the Catafract Cavalry, at Morbium [*Piercebridge?*]

[22]   Prefect of the Unit of Tigris Boatmen, at Arbeia [*South Shields*]

[23]   Prefect of the Unit of Nervii of Dictum, at Dictum [*Wearmouth?*]

[24]   Prefect of the Unit of Vigiles at Concangii [*Chester-le-Street*]

[25]   Prefect of the Unit of Exploratores, at Lavatrae [*Bowes*]

[26]   Prefect of the Unit of Directores, at Verterae [*Brough under Stainmore*]

[27]   Prefect of the Unit of Defensores, at Bravoniacum [*Kirkby Thore*]

[28]   Prefect of the Unit of Solenses, at Maglo [*Old Carlisle*]

[29]   Prefect of the Unit of Pacenses, at Magis [*Burrow Walls?*]

[30]   Prefect of the Unit of Longovicani, at Longovicium [*Lanchester*]

[31]   Prefect of the Unit of Supervenientes of Petuaria, at Derventio [*Malton?*]

[32] Also, along the line of the Wall:

[33]   Tribune of the Fourth Cohort of Lingones, at Segedunum [*Wallsend*]

[34]   Tribune of the First Cohort of Cornovii, at Pons Aelius [*Newcastle-upon-Tyne*]

[35]   Prefect of the First Ala of Asturians at Condercum [*Benwell*]

[36]   Tribune of the First Cohort of Frisiavones, at Vindobala [*Rudchester*]

[37]   Prefect of the Ala Sabiniana, at Hunnum [*Halton Chesters*]

[38]   Prefect of the Second Ala of Asturians, at Cilurnum [*Chesters*]

[39]   Tribune of the First Cohort of Batavians, at Procolitia [*Carrawburgh*]

[40]   Tribune of the First Cohort of Tungrians, at Borcovicium [*Housesteads*]

[41]   Tribune of the Fourth Cohort of Gauls, at Vindolan(d)a [*Chesterholm*]

[42]   Tribune of the First Cohort of Asturians, at Aesica [*Great Chesters*]

[43]   Tribune of the Second Cohort of Dalmatians, at Magna [*Carvoran*]

[44]   Tribune of the First Cohort of Hadrian's Own Dacians, at Camboglanna
         [*Castlesteads; perhaps an error for* Banna, *Birdoswald?*]

[45]   Prefect of the Ala Petriana, at Petriana [*Stanwix*]

[47]   Tribune of the Unit of Aurelian Moors, at Aballaba [*Burgh-by-Sands*]

[48]   Tribune of the Second Cohort of Lingones, at Congavata [*Drumburgh*]

[49]   Tribune of the First Cohort of Spaniards, at Axelodunum [*Netherby?*]

[50]   Tribune of the Second Cohort of Thracians, at Gabrosentum [*Moresby*]

[51]   Tribune of the First Cohort Aelia Classica, at Tunnocelum [*Beckermet?*

[52]   Tribune of the First Cohort of Morini, at Glannibanta [*Ravenglass*]

[53]   Tribune of the Third Cohort of Nervii, at Alione [*Lancaster?*]

[54]   The Cavalry Unit of Sarmatians, at Bremetennacum [*Ribchester*]

[55]   Prefect of the First Ala Herculea, at Olenacum [*Elslack?*]

[56]   Tribune of the Sixth Cohort of Nervii, at Virosidum [*Brough by Bainbridge?*]

     ([57–65] *list the administrative staff of the Duke*)

Z2.2.   Chapter 28, the Count of the Saxon Shore in Britain:

[12] Under the control of the *vir spectabilis*, the Count of the Saxon Shore
in the Britains:

[13]   Prefect of the Unit of Fortenses, at Othona [*Bradwell-on-Sea*]

[14]   Praepositus of the Tungrecanian Infantry, at Dubrae [*Dover*]

[15]   Praepositus of the Unit of Turnacenses, at Lemanae [*Lympne*]

[16]   Praepositus of the Dalmatian Cavalry of Branodunum, at Branodunum
                                                              [*Brancaster*]

[17]   Praepositus of the Stablesian Cavalry of Gariannonum, at Gariannonum
                                                              [*Burgh Castle*]

[18]   Tribune of the First Cohort of Baetasii, at Regulbium [*Reculver*]

[19]   Prefect of the Second Legion Augusta, at Rutupiae [*Richborough*]

[20]   Praepositus of the Unit of Abulci, at Anderidos [*Pevensey*]

[21]   Praepositus of the Unit of *Exploratores*, at Portus Adurni [*Portchester*]
          ([22–31] *list the administrative staff of the Count*)

Z2.3.   Chapter 29, the Count of the Britains;
             [*The officers and troops under his command are not listed, but the units
                 occur in an earlier chapter:*]
             Chapter 7, the Distribution of Units:

[153] With the *vir spectabilis*, the Count of the Britains:

[154]   Victores Juniores Britanniciani

[155]   Primani Juniores

[156]   Secundani Juniores

[199] In Britain with the *vir spectabilis*, the Count of the Britains:

[200]   Equites Catafractarii Juniores

[201]   Equites Scutarii Aureliaci

[202]   Equites Honoriani Seniores

[203]   Equites Stablesiani

[204]   Equites Syri

[205]   Equites Taifali

The *Notitia Dignitatum* ('List of Offices') is a register of all the officials, officers and military units in the Roman Empire, basically as it was when it was divided into East and West in AD 395, but with some updating into the early fifth century. It survives in four Renaissance copies of a now lost 9th-century manuscript, which was illustrated in colour with (mostly imaginary) badges for each official and shields for each unit.

Vir spectabilis ('The Admirable Man') was a late fourth-century title for men of senatorial rank holding important offices.

INDEX

Emperors (not necessarily at the time of the reference) and pretenders are shown in capitals with the dates of their reign. Romans are arranged by their family name, but cross-references are given for men usually known by another name. The standard abbreviation 'cos' is used when giving the date of a consulship.

Places only mentioned in the Notitia Dignitatum (Z) *are not indexed here.*

A LIST OF EMPERORS

(SIMPLIFIED AND NOT COMPREHENSIVE!)

	Julius Caesar (not emperor)	
31 BC – AD 14	Augustus	
AD 14 – 37	Tiberius	
AD 37 – 41	Gaius (Caligula)	JULIO-CLAUDIANS
AD 41 – 54	Claudius	
AD 54 – 68	Nero	
AD 69	'Year of the 4 emperors' (Galba, Otho, Vitellius, Vespasian)	
AD 69 – 79	Vespasian	
AD 79 – 81	Titus	FLAVIANS
AD 81 – 96	Domitian	
AD 96 – 98	Nerva	
AD 98 – 117	Trajan	
AD 117 – 138	Hadrian	CHOSEN & ADOPTED BY PREDECESSOR
AD 138 – 161	Antoninus Pius	
AD 161 – 180	Marcus Aurelius	
AD 180 – 192	Commodus (co-emperor from 177)	
AD 192 – 193	Pertinax and civil wars	
AD 193 – 211	Septimius Severus	
AD 198 – 217	Antoninus (Caracalla): co-emperor 198–211	
AD 217 – 218	Macrinus (not a Severan)	SEVERANS
AD 218 – 222	Elagabalus	
AD 222 – 235	Severus Alexander	

AD 235 – 284   'Third-century Crisis' over 20 emperors, some in power very briefly or over part of the empire only, including Postumus AD 260–268 'Gallic' Empire (Britain, Gaul, Spain, Germany).

AD 284 – 305   Diocletian establishes 'tetrarchy' with empire split into East and West with a 'senior emperor', *Augustus* and 'junior emperor', *Caesar* for each half. Pretenders still frequent, *e.g.* Carausius, AD 287–293 and Allectus, AD 293 – 296 'emperors' in Britain and N. Gaul.

AD 293 – 306	Constantius I Chlorus	
AD 306 – 337	Constantine I (the Great)	
AD 337 – 350	Constans I (co-emperor with brother, Constantius II)	DYNASTY OF CONSTANTIUS
AD 337 – 361	Constantius II (co-emperor with brother, Constans I)	
AD 361 – 363	Julian (Caesar for Britain and Gaul, 355–361)	

AD 364 – 375   Valentinian I (Augustus for West: brother, Valens, Augustus for East)

AD 375 – 383   Gratian (junior Augustus (West) from 367, then senior Augustus (West))

AD 379 – 395   Theodosius (senior Augustus for East from 379, sole Augustus from 392)

AD 395 – 423   Honorius (senior Augustus for West), faced revolts in Britain from Gratian (AD 407) and Constantine III 'emperor' for Britain and Gaul AD 407 – 411.